Harvard Economic Studies, Volume 143

Awarded the David A. Wells Prize for the year 1971–72 and published from the income of the David A. Wells Fund.

The studies in this series are published under the direction of the Department of Economics of Harvard University. The Department does not assume responsibility for the views expressed.

Market Signaling: Informational Transfer in Hiring and Related Screening Processes

A. Michael Spence

Harvard University Press, Cambridge, Massachusetts, 1974

Preface

I owe many people debts of gratitude for various kinds of help in developing the ideas set forth in this essay. I extend my thanks to Roy Radner and the members of the summer workshop on markets and uncertainty at Berkeley in 1971 for financial support and helpful comment, to the Ford Foundation for a research grant, to the members of the Seminar on Analytic Methods in Public Policy in the Kennedy School of Government at Harvard for intellectual, financial and moral support, and to the Department of Labor for aid in the typing and preparation of the manuscript.

I want especially to thank Holly Grano, Margo Sweet, Mary Beth Learnard, and Diane Lamping for editing and typing a difficult essay and for improving its style considerably in the process, and to express my appreciation to Charles Untiet for the index and a careful reading of the text.

Ann Spence, my wife, counsels students at Harvard on finding jobs and graduate schools. Much of what is written here is a response to accounts of her experience with problems that students face in these markets.

From the outset, I have enjoyed the benefit of talking with an astonishingly large group of people whose interests have carried them along similar paths and whose work should be read. David Starrett gave me valuable help with the basic concepts and much encouragement in the process. Jerry Green helped me with dynamics, and he has written several essays on stochastic price equilibria and incomplete intertemporal markets. Randy Weiss' insightful comments were based on his own research into returns to education. I owe a special debt to Michael Rothschild, whose essays on imperfect information and whose persistent interest in this work have been enormously stimulating.

Lester Telser and George Stigler ran a conference on the economics of information and gave me considerable help. Zvi Griliches read and criticized the entire manuscript and raised the issue of efficiency, an issue with which I have attempted to deal.

I had the benefit of a very interesting day at the National Bureau of Economic Research, where several people are carrying on related research. My thanks to James Heckman, Jacob Mincer, Bob Nelson, and Barry Chiswick.

Howard Raiffa is responsible for whatever I know about decision theory. In addition, the extremely high standard of expositional clarity which he imposes on his own work is a source of inspiration, and occasionally frustration, for those like me, who inevitably fall short of it. Richard Caves read the entire manuscript with a critical eye and showed me several places where analogous problems arise in the theory of industrial organization.

My greatest intellectual debts are to Kenneth Arrow, Thomas Schelling, and Richard Zeckhauser, whose help and encouragement extend back to my first days in graduate school. This type of debt is never repaid, nor even well expressed, but is, with luck, partially passed on to others who may someday need the stimulation by exposure and patient personal direction which I needed and received from these three teachers.

A. Michael Spence
Stanford University, 1973

Contents

Appendices

Figures

Tables

Market Signaling

1 Introduction

Market signals are activities or attributes of individuals in a market which, by design or accident, alter the beliefs of, or convey information to, other individuals in the market. Thus broadly defined, the subject is too large for one book-length study. Although advertisements, brand names, and prices are sometimes market signals, I have found it necessary to restrict the analysis to what might be called the job market or hiring paradigm. It is difficult to convey an accurate impression of the meaning of the term and the scope of economic activity to which it is intended to refer, in abstraction from the sorts of examples which are the focus of the analysis of most of the book. In short, the reader and I have a signaling problem. We are engaged in a signaling game with a reasonably complicated incentive structure. To read further is to invest in a commodity of uncertain quality, much as the purchaser of a consumer durable is investing in an uncertain flow of services over time, when he buys the good. The seller of the consumer durable and I may attempt to send signals to our respective customers to create a favorable impression or, more precisely, to affect the consumer's subjective probabilistic beliefs about the quality of our products. We will do this even if the product has very little to recommend it.

Our problem arises from the fact that the consumer, knowing our interest in the matter, will rightly discount our signals rather heavily. And yet perhaps not totally. General Electric and I expect to be in our respective markets for some time to come, and hence there may be some merit in considering the long-run benefits of investing now in our future abilities to communicate via the establishment of our signaling credibility. To do so would not be to act without precedent. Ski resorts have long engaged in reporting ski conditions to the public. The reports are not totally inaccurate and are broadcast on the media, at no cost to the resort. Of course, the signaling game is played every week.[1]

If the reader believed that an author would be in the market only once, or, at best, at infrequent intervals, the argument that the author might invest in signaling credibility by accurately reporting the contents of this volume would carry much less weight. The primary focus of this book is a class of market phenomena which have this last characteristic, that the primary signalers are in the game sufficiently infrequently that they are believed not to invest, and, in fact, do not invest, in acquiring a signaling reputation and in establishing a learnable signaling code. The paradigm case of this type of market signaling situation may be found in job markets. And it is toward signaling in the context of screening people that a large portion of the analysis here is devoted.

The goal is to construct models which capture what seem to be important aspects of the process of communication and information transfer in job markets. The premise upon which the analysis is based is that the employer, in most hiring situations, is uncertain about the productive capabilities of the job applicant prior to hiring him, and usually for some period of time after hiring. Hiring is investing under uncertainty. That employers are uncertain is an instance of the general proposition that buyers are often uncertain about the properties of the commodity at the time of buying. Those who have had occasion to

---

1. For a discussion of conventionally based market signaling, see the concluding section of this book. More generally, see D. K. Lewis, *Convention: A Philosophical Study* (Cambridge, Mass.: Harvard University Press, 1969).

have their automobiles repaired or serviced may find a certain merit in this proposition.

Although the employer (or, in another comparable context, the college admissions officer) does not know all that he would like to know at the time of making his decision, he is not totally in the dark, either. He confronts a plethora of potential signals in the form of observable attributes of the individual, ranging from personal appearance to education, employment record (if any), other aspects of personal history, and race and sex. These signals will be interpreted by the employer in the light of his past experience in the market.

The individual exercises some control over the image he projects to the prospective employer, and presumably he will manipulate this image to create favorable impressions. These strategic decisions may involve relatively small-scale activities, like buying and wearing a new suit, or more considerable decisions such as acquiring or extending one's education. Other aspects of the image one presents are, of course, beyond one's control. Race and sex are examples.

One can be interested in this type of signaling for several reasons, summarized in the following questions:

1. Is there a reasonable concept of signaling equilibrium, and how is it characterized?

2. How well or badly informed are employers in the market?

3. Are information flows complete? Are they accurate?

4. Does signaling use resources, and, if so, does it use them efficiently?

5. What are the informational roles played by alterable and unalterable aspects of the image the applicant presents?

6. What learning takes place?

7. Does uncertainty disappear in a market equilibrium situation?

8. How many equilibria are there?

9. Given uncertainty, imperfect information, and signaling activity, does the market perform its allocative functions efficiently?

This is a sample of the questions to which one would want answers from models of market signaling. Without serious risk of exaggeration, I believe the reader will find some of the answers surprising and perhaps a little disquieting from the point of view of the allocative efficiency of the market.

Although job markets are the focus of attention, they are intended to be illustrative of a certain kind of market signaling structure which appears in other markets and quasimarkets. These can be viewed through the same conceptual lens. One such case has already been mentioned: college admissions. Along the same lines, selective screening and promotion can usefully be viewed in terms of signaling. Credit ratings and the market for household loans will receive some attention. Expenditures for the purpose of acquiring status, a phenomenon first suggested by Veblen, is an interesting variant of the same model. In the course of our investigation, these and other cases are examined.[2]

A word about the organization of the essay is in order. In developing the job market model, examining its properties, and then using it to examine similar signaling phenomena, I have made extensive use of numerical examples to illustrate important points. No mathematical sophistication beyond the level of simple algebra is required. The same cannot be said of the appendices, where the numerical examples are extended and generalized. The exception is Appendix E on efficiency, which can be read independently of the rest. The appendices are a necessary adjunct to the text; they show that the properties of the simpler examples of market signaling are reasonably general and not contrived, and they extend the substance of the analysis.

I hope to have solved the signaling problem mentioned at the outset, to have given the reader some flavor of the subject matter and the type of investigation conducted here, and, at the same time, not to have been misleading. After the examination of one market signaling game in detail is complete, it will be easier to generalize and reflect upon market signaling in the abstract.

2. These examples are meant to be illustrative of the fact that the job market model is found in other places; they do not represent a complete list.

2 Job Market Signaling

When uncertainty and information are a part of the problem one is analyzing, there is the possibility that people are learning, revising their beliefs, and responding differently in the market. Yet a continual state of flux is difficult to deal with, and it becomes reasonable to look for an appropriate equilibrium concept. For purposes of the job market, an equilibrium might be defined as a situation in which employers' beliefs about the relationship between productivity (which cannot be known at the time of hiring) and education, job experience, race, and sex are confirmed by the results of his hiring in the market. Using the concept of equilibrium, so defined, will yield insights into the efficiency (or lack of efficiency) implicit in the use of a market system for allocating jobs to people and people to jobs.

It is argued here that the informational structure of the market is crucial to the performance of that market, that information flows are the output of a signaling game, and that the incentive structure of the signaling game is an integral part of the incentive structure of the market itself. It is further argued that signaling equilibria, far from being unique, are many; that they are not equivalent from the point of view of social welfare; that there are likely to be differences between private and social returns to education, because education is used as a signal; and that there are several qualitatively distinct potential sources of economic discrimination implicit in the market's informational structure.

Transactions in the Job Market

The typical transaction in a labor market is two-sided. Each party to the transaction buys something, and each sells something else. The employee sells his labor services, usually for a specified period of time, and buys a job or job description and a work environment. The employer buys the labor services, or, more accurately, he buys a lottery whose outcome is the actual labor service he receives, and he sells the job and the work environment. Wages or salaries are the net transfers which result from such two-way sales. Depending upon which side of the transaction one is looking at, the market is referred to as a labor market or a job market.

When the employer and potential employee confront each other in the market (the confrontation may be preceded by a considerable amount of search by either party or both), neither is certain about the qualities or characteristics of the service which the other is offering for sale. The potential employee may not know exactly what the job will be like, and the employer frequently does not know how effectively the job applicant will do the job if he or she is hired. The focus of attention here is the uncertainty of the employer, which stems from the fact that he does not know, prior to hiring, how productive a particular employee will turn out to be; this is because the employer cannot directly observe productivity prior to hiring.

By limiting the essay in this way, I am ignoring several other aspects of the informational structure of the market. One is the employee's uncertainty about the job. Another is the fact that employers and employees have to find each other in the market. The latter may result in search procedures by either one or both of them. In slighting these informational problems, I do not mean to suggest that they are unimportant. But for this investigation, I am interested not in the entire labor market, but rather in a certain kind of market signaling game, one version of which is found in job markets.

Employer Uncertainty and Responses to It

The extent and nature of the employer's uncertainty will vary from market to market and from job to job. But it would be hard to deny that employer uncertainty is a pervasive feature of situations in which someone's labor services are being purchased. The competence and creativity of the corporate manager, for example, cannot be accurately predicted beforehand, which is not to say that there are no indicators that may help in making the prediction. On the contrary, the presence of such indicators is the subject of investigation. Anyone who has had an automobile repaired will know that the quality of the workmanship and the honesty of the establishment are both uncertain and matters of concern. In hiring for skilled jobs, the employer may rely heavily upon a union or guild to help him assess the qualifications of an individual, and even then he may be uncertain. And the layman who purchases the services of a doctor has very little notion of the precise quality of the service. In short, the typical purchaser of a labor service, be he an individual or a large organization, is almost always uncertain about the service he is buying and hence, in making the purchase, he is really acquiring a lottery. A lottery is simply a chance to receive one of a collection of payoffs, rewards, or consequences. The probability attached to each outcome may be some objectively defined quantity, or it may be a subjective quantity, supplied by the holder of the lottery. The important point is that people can buy and sell lotteries just as they can buy and sell goods and services. We can therefore talk in terms of the market for certain kinds of lotteries.

The lottery which the employer thinks he is buying is defind both in terms of the possible outcomes — in this case, varying degrees of competence in the performance of the job by the employee — and in terms of the probabilities he attaches to each of these outcomes. We need linger only briefly over the outcomes themselves. It seems reasonable to assume that the employer will have a lively sense for the range of possible consequences, based upon his past experience in the market. The individual may turn out to be superbly imaginative and creative, merely competent, incompetent, dishonest, punctual or always late, frequently absent, and so on. How important each of these factors is depends upon the type of job and the hiring organization itself.

The interesting question, then, concerns the probabilities that the employer attaches to the various possible outcomes of hiring the individual (which in the present terminology means purchasing a lottery). In attaching probabilities to these outcomes, the employer has two resources. One is his past experience in the market (we shall assume that he has been in the market for some time). He does not simply have to make unaided guesses at the probabilities. His experience should tell him something, since he will have a sense for the frequency with which different outcomes have occurred in the past.

The other factor is that people are not indistinguishable. They come with various types of education and job experience, they come dressed differently, with different hair lengths, and of different sexes and races. Thus, although the employer does not know what he would really like to know about the individual, he does have a quantity of potentially useful information in the form of observable characteristics of individual applicants. And he may try to use this information in making his probability assessments. Instead of estimating the unconditional probability that an applicant, drawn randomly from the applicant pool, will be competent, he can estimate the *conditional* probability of competence, given the observable characteristics of the individual who is applying for the job. Both types of estimates are made on the basis of past experience.

It is not certain that the use of conditional probabilities to evaluate the lottery will result in better decisions. In fact, it has not yet been demonstrated that the conditional and unconditional probabilities will differ at all. It may be that in the historical sample, education and productivity are uncorrelated. One can say, however, that provided there are no costs to digesting this "additional information," using it cannot result in worse decisions. The reason is that the information, if indeed it is useless, will be discarded in the process of making the decision.[1]

The reader will realize that the term "characteristic" is used loosely to refer to all those facts about the individual to which the employer has access prior to hiring. These include education levels, job history, personal characteristics, and other things like service record and criminal record. Since all these are (or may be) observable, they are potential sources of information. That is to say, they potentially affect the employer's probabilistic beliefs. The simple distinction between characteristics which are observable and those which are not might be further refined. There may be observation costs. If there are, the employer faces a sequential decision problem of what to observe and in what order. For expositional clarity, observation costs are suppressed in favor of the dichotomy.

Employee Signaling

Of those characteristics which are observable to the employer prior to hiring, some are subject to manipulation by the individual, and others are not. Education can be acquired and educational performance improved. Race and sex, on the other hand, are not subject to adjustment. Note that it is possible (and may be desirable) to make observable, unalterable characteristics like race and sex unobservable. To do so would probably involve an institutional or a social decision. Colleges, for example, are forbidden in many states to seek to acquire information about an applicant's race, color, religion, or national origin. There are obvious difficulties in designing effective disguises. But suppressing the observability of a characteristic does not make it adjustable. The importance of the distinction will shortly be made clear.

Since some potentially relevant characteristics such as educa-

1. In the language of decision theory, the expected value of sample information is at least zero (ignoring sampling costs).

tion are partially or completely controllable by the individual, it is reasonable to assume that an applicant will make those adjustments which make him or her appear in a favorable light in the eyes of potential employers. The individual can and does affect the lottery he presents to the employer by altering some of his observable characteristics, although he need not think of himself as projecting an image. It is assumed that these adjustments are the product of rational decisions. The activity will be referred to as *signaling* and the characteristics themselves will be called *signals*. The term *index* will be reserved for observable unalterable characteristics. In addition, it is useful to distinguish potential and actual signals and indices as follows:

    1. A *potential signal* is an observable alterable characteristic.

    2. A *potential index* is an observable unalterable characteristic.

    3. An *actual signal* is a potential signal which affects an employer's conditional probability assessments of productivity.

    4. An *actual index* is a potential index which affects an employer's conditional probability assessments of productivity.

In adopting this terminology, I am following the spirit of the distinction drawn by Robert Jervis in his excellent book, *The Logic of Images in International Relations.* Jervis uses the index-signal dichotomy to analyze how nations communicate. The dichotomy stands for a number of finer distinctions which we can use here. The primary distinction is between manipulable and nonmanipulable characteristics or attributes or activities. A second is between activities of which the sender is aware and those of which he is not. The notion is that if he is not aware of them, then he will not manipulate them; thus, they function as indices. Great emphasis is laid by Jervis upon the effectiveness of discovering activities which are being taken as indices and then using them to mislead the other party. One can distinguish voluntary and involuntary activities. Involuntary activities are indices; voluntary ones may be signals if the actor is aware of their signaling potential. One can also distinguish high- and low-cost signals. The notion here is that very high-cost signals are effectively indices, since no one would consider manipulating them purely for the purpose of communication.

Examples of this will be encountered later in the discussion of credit markets.

Jervis' conceptual distinctions are richer than I have been able to convey here in a short space. Considerable complications arise when one considers whether parties to the signaling game are aware that the other thinks of an activity as a signal or an index.[2] Nevertheless, the spirit of the signal-index dichotomy is maintained. A signal is a manipulable attribute or activity which conveys information, and the activity is called signaling. The only modification is that in general it is not necessary to insist that the actor, in manipulating the attribute, think of himself as signaling or conveying information. Unalterable attributes are called indices. The perspiration on the forehead of the nervous job applicant is an index.

It should be noted that whether or not potential signals and indices turn out to be actual, that is to say, to affect employers' assessments of productivity, is a property of a market equilibrium and is not something which can be decided in advance.

Model 1: The No-Signaling Case

A brief examination of the case in which no signaling takes place will serve as a standard of comparison. Let us assume there is just one employer and a collection of people whom he will ultimately hire. Each person has a marginal product or net worth to the employer, but the employer does not know what this marginal productivity is prior to hiring. For expositional purposes, let us assume there are just two possible values for an individual's productivity: one or two. In a world of perfect information, the employer would pay each person exactly his

2. An interesting use of similar concepts is found in Erving Goffman, *Strategic Interaction,* in which the author devotes considerable attention to the communication problems of spies. See also G. Perrault, *The Red Orchestra* (New York: Simon and Schuster, 1969), on the Soviet spy network in Europe during World War II.

marginal product.[3] We shall assume that the proportion of people who have a marginal product of one is q_1, while the remainder have a marginal product of two (see Table 2.1).

Table 2.1. Market Data for the No-Signaling Case

	Marginal product	Proportion of the population
Group I	1	q_1
Group II	2	$1 - q_1$

If everyone looks alike in all relevant respects — and this means that on the basis of the employer's past experience in the market, observable differences among them are uncorrelated with their productive capabilities — then the employer will pay each person his expected marginal product. This expected marginal product is the same for all people because of the absence of signals and indices; it is computed to be

$$w = q_1 + 2(1 - q_1) = 2 - q_1.$$

As compared with the hypothetical world of perfect information, the members of Group I are better off by virtue of being initially indistinguishable from higher-productivity people. The members of Group II are hurt. The extent of the benefit to the individual in Group I is equal to $1 - q_1$ and hence increases as q_1 falls. The damage to the individual in Group II is $-q_1$ and increases as q_1 increases. The employer is indifferent between the two worlds, since the amount of work done and the total wage bills are the same in each.

If better information were available, however, it is assumed the employer would make use of it. For we must imagine (and

3. With the reader's indulgence, I should like to postpone a more detailed consideration of competitive pressure in a market with imperfect information and signaling until the appendices, particularly D and E. In the meantime, I shall use one-employer models for expositional purposes.

the reader is asked to imagine) that the employer is embedded in a world in which there are at least some competitive pressures in the labor market. His failure to use better information when others are using it would mean that he would be unable to compete for the talented people.

3 Model 2: Education as a Signal

With the no-signaling model as a backdrop, the first model of market signaling can be outlined. Let us suppose that education is available as a potential signal. Individuals have different numbers of years of education and different levels of performance in education. The employer has access to these prior to hiring.

At this point, one might ask why the employer would not simply hire the person, determine his productivity, and then either fire him or adjust his wage or salary accordingly. There are several reasons why he will not do this. Frequently, he cannot. It may take time (even a long time) for the individual's real capabilities to become apparent. There may be a specific training required before the individual can handle certain kinds of jobs. There may be a contract and a contract period within which the individual cannot be fired and his salary cannot be adjusted. All of these factors tend to make the hiring decision an investment decision for the employer. Certain costs incurred in hiring and in the early period of employment are sunk and cannot be recovered if the investment turns out badly. The employer, therefore, is likely to pay attention to potential signals.

For individuals, education is a matter of choice. The individual can and does invest in years of education and in his performance in education. There are costs, both monetary and psychic, to acquiring an education and a good educational record. The problem for the individual who faces wage, salary, and job schedules that may depend on education is to select an optimal level of education, keeping in mind both the costs and potential benefits in terms of his future job and salary level.

A Critical Assumption or Prerequisite

At this point, a critical assumption is necessary. Let us assume that education is measured by a composite index of years and performance, denoted by y. The critical assumption is that the costs of acquiring y are negatively correlated with the individual's productive capability with respect to some job. In particular, using the data of model 1 as our starting point, it is assumed that the costs of y for a Group I person are exactly y, while the costs of an educational level y for a person with a marginal product of two are $y/2$. The unit may be taken as dollars. Thus, the high-productivity types have lower educational costs than the others.

In the context of the model, the negative correlation of signaling costs and productive capability is an assumption. But actually it is a prerequisite for effective market signaling to take place in this type of market. The reader, therefore, may think of the assumption as a general prerequisite for a potential signal to be an actual signal. The point will come up again later.[1]

The Model

The story of the market signaling game can be interrupted at any one of a number of places. Let us start with the employer's beliefs about the relationship between education and productivity at some point in time (Table 3.1). The employer will have

1. More generally, if some alterable characteristic is to be an actual signal for productive capability in a market signaling equilibrium, then (a) it must be costly to adjust, and (b) the adjustment costs must be negatively correlated with productive capability. The validity of the proposition will be clearer after we have had a chance to define a market signaling equilibrium.

Table 3.1. Data of the Signaling Problem

Group	Marginal product	Proportion of population	Cost of education level Y
I	1	q_1	y
II	2	$1 - q_1$	$y/2$

conditional probabilities over productivity given educational levels at our arbitrary starting point. Using the conditional probabilities, he will have an expected marginal productivity for each possible level of education. It is assumed that he offers to pay anyone with y years of education the expected marginal productivity corresponding to this level of education. The latter is denoted by $W(y)$. It is the offered wage schedule to education levels.

The potential employee, looking forward to his working life, faces the schedule $W(y)$. This schedule tells him the payoff to be had from each choice of education level. There are also costs of education. Given the costs, and the payoffs, the individual will select a level of education which maximizes the difference between payoffs and costs. In other words, he maximizes the return net of signaling costs by choosing y appropriately.

If this were where the story ended, it would not be very interesting. But it does not end here. Applicants, having invested in education, go onto the market and are hired at the rates determined by the employer's current conditional probabilistic beliefs. In the period subsequent to hiring, the employer will learn about the actual productive capabilities of the people he has hired. He also knows the education levels they brought to the market. Putting these two types of information together, he can and will test his probabilistic beliefs concerning the relationship between productivity and education. In general, this newly acquired experience will cause him to alter his former beliefs. When this happens, the wages offered to people with various levels of education will change when the game starts again. This, in turn, will alter the investment behavior of individuals, and the new market data will cause further revisions in the employer's beliefs (Fig. 3.1).

To study situations that are not transitory, one looks for places at which the circular ebb and flow of the feedback mechanism settles down. Such places are referred to as equilibria. They will occur when the employer's beliefs feed back upon themselves in the form of market data which do not cause him to revise his beliefs any further. Beliefs having this property will be described as self-confirming.

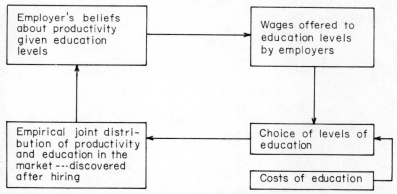

Figure 3.1. The Flow of Interrelationships in the Signaling Model

Definition: A signaling equilibrium in the market is a set of conditional probabilistic beliefs for the employer which, when translated into offered wages, employee investment responses, and new market data, are confirmed by the new market data relating education levels to productivity. New groups of entrants into the job market come into the market, but their investment in signals is similar to that of their predecessors, and the employer has no reason to adjust his conditional probabilities.

It is important to emphasize that this merely defines an equilibrium in the market. It has not been shown that an equilibrium exists, nor that education will be an actual signal — that the conditional and unconditional probabilities over productivity levels will differ. The properties of an equilibrium require investigation, as does the question whether one or many equilibria exist.

In order to find an equilibrium in the market, it is necessary to guess at a set of self-confirming conditional probabilistic beliefs for the employer and then determine whether they are in fact confirmed by the feedback mechanisms described above. Suppose that the employer believes that if $y < \bar{y}$, then productivity is one with probability one, and that if $y \geqslant \bar{y}$, then productivity will be two with probability one. If these are his conditional beliefs, then his offered wage schedule, $W(y)$, will be a step function (Fig. 3.2). Note that $\bar{y}$ is just some number for the time being.[2]

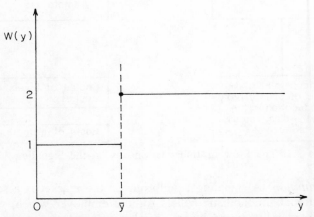

Figure 3.2. Offered Wages as a Function of Level of Education

Given the offered wage schedule, members of each group will select optimal levels for education. Consider the person who will set $y < \bar{y}$. If he does this, he will set $y = 0$, because education is costly and until he reaches $\bar{y}$, there are no benefits to increasing y, given the employer's hypothesized beliefs. Similarly, any individual who sets $y \geqslant \bar{y}$ will in fact set $y = \bar{y}$, since further increases would merely incur costs with no corresponding benefits. Everyone will therefore either set $y = 0$ or set

2. Statisticians, accustomed to using bars to denote means or averages, may be confused. The bar here has nothing to do with means or averages.

$y = \bar{y}$. Given the employer's initial beliefs and the fact just deduced, if the employer's beliefs are to be confirmed, then members of Group I must set $y = 0$, while members of Group II set $y = \bar{y}$. Diagrams of the options facing the two groups are shown in Fig. 3.3.

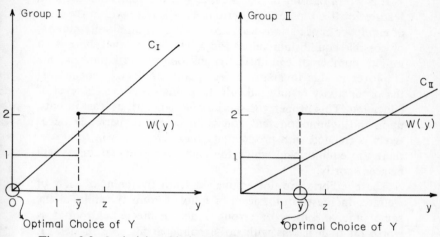

Figure 3.3. Optimizing Choice of Education for Both Groups

Superimposed upon the wage schedule are the cost schedules for the two groups. Each group selects y to maximize the difference between the offered wages and the costs of education. Given the level of $\bar{y}$ in the diagram, it is easy to see that Group I selects $y = 0$, and Group II sets $y = \bar{y}$. Thus, in this case, the employer's beliefs are confirmed, and we have a signaling equilibrium. We can state in algebraic terms the conditions on the behavior by the two groups that will confirm the employer's beliefs. Group I sets $y = 0$ if

$$1 > 2 - \bar{y}.$$

Group II will set $y = \bar{y}$ as required, provided that

$$2 - \bar{y}/2 > 1.$$

Putting these two conditions together, we find that the employer's initial beliefs are confirmed by market experience provided that $\bar{y}$ satisfies the inequality

$$1 < \bar{y} < 2.$$

It is worth pausing at this point to remark upon some striking features of this type of equilibrium. One is that, within the class of employer expectations used above, there is an infinite number of possible equilibrium values for $\bar{y}$. This means that there is an infinite number of equilibria. In any one of the equilibria, the employer is able to make perfect point predictions concerning the productivity of any individual, having observed his level of education. This property is special and depends, at least in part, upon the assumption that education costs are perfectly negatively correlated with productivity. However, even in this case, there are equilibria in which the employer is uncertain, as will be seen shortly.

The equilibria are not equivalent from the point of view of welfare. Increases in the level of $\bar{y}$ hurt Group II, while, at the same time, members of Group I are unaffected. Group I is worse off than it was with no signaling at all (see model 1). Group II may also be worse off than it was with no signaling. Assume that the proportion of people in Group I is 0.5. Since $\bar{y} > 1$, and the net return to the member of Group II is $2 - \bar{y}/2$, in equilibrium, his net return must be below 1.5, the no-signaling wage. Thus, everyone would prefer a situation in which there is no signaling.

No one is acting irrationally as an individual. Coalitions might profitably form and upset the signaling equilibrium; coalitions and groups are discussed in a later section. The initial proportions of people in the two groups, q_1 and $1 - q_1$, have no effect upon the equilibrium. This conclusion depends upon the assumption that the marginal product of a person in a given group does not change with numbers hired. Notice, however, that the no-signaling wage does depend upon q_1 under the same assumption.

Given the signaling equilibrium, the education level $\bar{y}$, which defines the equilibrium, is an entrance requirement or pre-requisite for the high-salary job — or so it would appear from the outside. From the point of view of the individual, it is a prerequisite. It has its source in a signaling game. Looked at from the outside, education might appear to be productive. It is productive for the individual, but, in this example, it does not increase his real marginal product at all.

Although we have assumed that education is unproductive, that is not essential to the model. Consider, for example, the modified situation in Table 3.2.

Table 3.2. Market Data with Education Being Productive

	Marginal product	Proportion of the population	Education costs
Group I	$1 + y/4$	q_1	y
Group II	$2 + y/4$	$1 - q_1$	$y/2$

We assume that the form of the employer's beliefs are as before: if $y < \bar{y}$, productivity is $1 + y/4$ with certainty; if $y \geqslant \bar{y}$, productivity is $2 + y/4$ with probability one. For an equilibrium, Group I sets $y = 0$, and Group II sets $y = \bar{y}$. This will confirm the employer's beliefs. Group I will make the requisite choice provided that

$$1 > 2 + \bar{y}/4 - \bar{y},$$

while Group II will set $y = \bar{y}$ provided that

$$2 + \bar{y}/4 - \bar{y}/2 > 1.$$

Therefore, we find the employer's beliefs are confirmed in the market, provided that

$$4/3 < \bar{y} < 4.$$

Notice that in Table 3.3 the pattern of the signaling equilibrium is similar in all respects to that found in the earlier case, with ed-

Table 3.3. Outcome of the Signaling Game

	Education level	Wage	Return net of signaling costs
Group I	$y = 0$	1	1
Group II	$y = \bar{y}$	$2 + \bar{y}/4$	$2 - \bar{y}/4$

ucation unproductive. The social and private returns to education are quite different. If one were to estimate social return to education by comparing wages and various levels of education in the labor force, one might seriously overestimate the contribution of education to output in the economy.

A sophisticated objection to the assertion that private and social returns differ might be that, in the context of our example, the social return is not really zero. We have an information problem in the society, as well as the problem of allocating the right people to the right jobs. Education, in its capacity as a signal in the model, is helping us to do this properly. The objection is well founded.[3] To decide how efficient or inefficient this system is, one must consider the realistic alternatives to market-sorting procedures in the society. But even within the confines of the market model, there are more or less efficient ways of getting the sorting accomplished. Increases in $\bar{y}$ improve the quality of the sorting not one bit. They simply use up real or psychic resources. This is just another way of saying that there are Pareto inferior signaling equilibria in the market.

It is not always the case that all groups lose because of the existence of signaling. For example, if, in the signaling equilibrium, $\bar{y} < 2q_1$, then Group II would be better off when education is functioning effectively as a signal than it would be otherwise. Thus, in the example, if $q_1 > 1/2$, so that Group II is a minority, then there exists a signaling equilibrium in which the members of Group II improve their position over the no-

3. I am indebted to Zvi Griliches and George Stigler for drawing this fact to my attention. I want to make it clear that the fact that there are inefficient signaling equilibria is in no way an argument for suppressing the signaling activity altogether. Appendix E deals more comprehensively with the efficiency question.

signaling case. Recall that the wage in the no-signaling case was a uniform $2 - q_1$ over all groups.

This bit of analysis can be generalized slightly. Suppose that the signaling cost schedule for Group I were given by $a_1 y$ and that for Group II by $a_2 y$. Then a small amount of calculation shows that there is a signaling equilibrium in which Group II is better off than with no signaling, provided that

$$q_1 > a_2/a_1.$$

How small a "minority" Group II has to be to have the possibility of benefiting from signaling depends upon the ratio of the marginal signaling cost of the two groups.

The calculation is straightforward. Given these signaling costs, groups will make the requisite choice to confirm the employer's beliefs provided that

$$1 > 2 - a_1\bar{y},$$

and

$$2 - a_2\bar{y} > 1.$$

These translate easily into the following condition on $\bar{y}$:

$$1/a_1 < \bar{y} < 1/a_2.$$

Now, if Group II is to be better off for some signaling equilibrium, then it must be better off with $\bar{y}$ as small as possible. Thus

$$2 - a_2/a_1 > 2 - q_1,$$

or

$$q_1 > a_2/a_1.$$

It is worth noting that there are other equilibria in the system with quite different properties. Suppose that the employer's expectations are of the following form.

If $y < \bar{y}$: Group I with probability q_1
Group II with probability $1 - q_1$
If $y \gtrless \bar{y}$: Group II with probability 1.

As before, the only levels of y which could conceivably be selected are $y = 0$ and $y = \bar{y}$. The wage for $y = 0$ is $2 - q_1$, while the wage for $y = \bar{y}$ is simply 2. From Fig. 3.4 it is easy to see that both groups rationally set $y = 0$, provided that $\bar{y} > 2q_1$. If they both do this, then the employer's beliefs are confirmed, and the market is in an equilibrium.

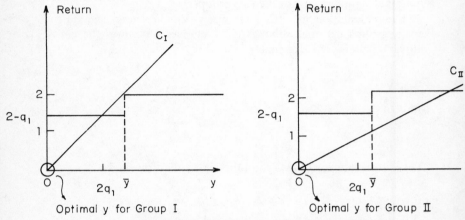

Figure 3.4. Optimal Signaling Decisions for the Two Groups

The employer's beliefs about the relationship between productivity and education for $y \gtrless \bar{y}$ are confirmed in a somewhat degenerate but perfectly acceptable sense. There are no data at all relating to these levels of education and hence, by logic, no disconfirming data. This is an example of a phenomenon of much wider potential importance. The employer's beliefs may drive certain groups from the market and into another labor market. We cannot capture this in a simple one-employer, one-market model. But when it happens, there is no experience forthcoming to the employer to cause him to alter his beliefs. I shall return to this point in a later section.

Education conveys no information in this type of equilibrium. In fact, we have reproduced the wages and information state of the employer in the no-signaling model as a signaling equilibrium.

Just as there exists a signaling equilibrium in which everyone sets $y = 0$, there is also an equilibrium in which everyone sets $y = \bar{y}$ for some positive $\bar{y}$. The requisite employer beliefs are

If $y < \bar{y}$: Group I with probability 1
If $y \geq \bar{y}$: Group I with probability q_1
Group II with probability $1 - q_1$.

Following our familiar mode of analysis, one finds that these beliefs are self-confirming in the market, provided that

$$\bar{y} < 1 - q_1.$$

Again, the education level conveys no useful information, but, in this instance, individuals are rationally investing in education. If they did not invest, they would incur lower wages, and the loss would exceed the gain from not making the educational investment. The implication of this version of the signaling equilibrium is that there can be stable prerequisites for jobs which convey no information by virtue of their existence, and hence serve no function.[4]

It is interesting to note that this last possibility does not depend upon costs being correlated with productivity at all. Suppose that the signaling costs for both groups were given by the one schedule y. And suppose further that employer beliefs were as described above. Then everyone will rationally select $y = \bar{y}$, provided that

$$\bar{y} < 1 - q_1.$$

---

4. For a discussion of this and related points, see Ivar Berg, *Education and Jobs: The Great Training Robbery* (Boston: Beacon Press, 1971).

The outcome is the same. But the interesting thing is that because of the absence of any correlation between educational costs and productivity, education could *never* be an effective signal, in the sense of conveying useful information, in an equilibrium in this market.

The model illustrates some of the effects the signaling game may have upon the allocational functioning of the market. The numerical example is not important. The potential effects and patterns of signaling are.

An alterable characteristic like education, which is a potential signal, becomes an actual signal if the signaling costs are negatively correlated with the individual's unknown productivity. Actually, the negative correlation is a necessary but not sufficient condition for signaling to take place. To see this in the context of our model, assume that the only values y can have are one and three. That is to say, you can only have units of education in lumps. If this is true, then there is no feasible value of $\bar{y}$ which will make it worthwhile for Group II to acquire an education. Three units are too much, and one unit will not distinguish Group II from Group I. Therefore, effective signaling depends upon not only the negative correlation of costs and productivities, but also upon there being a "sufficient" number of signals within the appropriate cost range.

An equilibrium is defined in the context of a feedback loop, in which employer expectations lead to wages offered to various levels of education, which in turn lead to investment in education by individuals. After hiring, the discovery of the actual relationships between education and productivity in the sample leads to revised expectations or beliefs. Here the cycle starts again. An equilibrium is best thought of as a set of beliefs which are confirmed or at least not contradicted by the new data at the end of the loop just described. Such beliefs will tend to persist over time as new entrants into the market flow through.

A question not considered thus far concerns what happens after the employer discovers the individual's productive capabilities. Presumably some sort of adjustment takes place, and the individual may return to the job markets in the economy.

At that point he begins a new game; however, his work history now becomes part of his observable bundle of characteristics, and one employer knows more about him than the others. Of course, he or she may stay with the initial employer. This process is capturable in a model with characteristics like the simple model we have been looking at. But the model is more general and more complicated.[5]

Multiple equilibria are a distinct possibility. Some may be Pareto inferior to others. Private and social returns to education diverge. Sometimes everyone loses as a result of the existence of signaling. In other situations, some gain while others lose. Systematic overinvestment in education is a distinct possibility because of the element of arbitrariness in the equilibrium configuration of the market. In the context of atomistic behavior (which has been assumed thus far), everyone is reacting rationally to the market situation. Information is passed to the employer through the education signal. In some of the examples, it was perfect information. In other cases, this is not so.[6] There will be random variation in signaling costs which prevent the employer from distinguishing perfectly among individuals of varying productive capabilities.

Education was measured by a scalar quantity in the examples. With no basic adjustment in the conceptual apparatus, we can think of education as a multidimensional quantity: years of education, institution attended, grades, recommendations, and so on. Similarly, it is not necessary to think in terms of two groups of people. There may be many groups, or even a continuum of people, some suited to certain kinds of work, others suited to others. Nor need education be strictly unproductive. As one example demonstrated, the same types of equilibrium signaling patterns may occur when education is productive.

5. See Appendix I, A Flow-through Model of Signaling and Job Choice.
6. In a later chapter on randomness in signaling costs, we find that an imperfect correlation between signaling costs and productive capabilities produces imperfect information to the employer. I have dealt with the less realistic case of perfect correlation here, for expositional clarity.

However, if it is too productive relative to the costs, everyone
will invest heavily in education, and education may cease to
have a signaling function.

A Continuous Example

The reader may suspect at this point that these somewhat unusual properties of equilibria depend upon contrived properties
of the examples. In particular, one might suspect that the multiple equilibria depend upon the discreteness in the values of
individual productivities. While I am relying on appendices to
demonstrate the generality of these signaling phenomena, it is
perhaps worthwhile to show briefly that continuous versions of
the same model have similar properties.

Let n stand for productivity, a quantity which varies continuously over the employable population. We shall assume that
the cost of education level y for the individual with productive
capability n is y/n. In equilibrium the employer will predict n
using y, with a function of the form

$$n = f(y). \qquad (3.1)$$

The task is to find an equilibrium $f(y)$. Assume some $f(y)$ is
given. The individual with productivity n will maximize return
net of signaling, $f(y) - y/n$, by setting

$$f'(y) = \frac{1}{n}. \qquad (3.2)$$

The second order condition is

$$f''(y) < 0. \qquad (3.3)$$

In equilibrium, it is necessary that $f(y)$ be an accurate prediction of n; that is, $n = f(y)$. Substituting in (3.2) for n, yields

$$f'(y) = \frac{1}{f(y)}. \tag{3.4}$$

Any function $f(y)$ that defines an equilibrium set of employer expectations satisfies the differential equation (3.4). The solution to (3.4) is a one parameter family of curves

$$f(y) = (2y + k)^{1/2}, \tag{3.5}$$

where k is the parameter. Any of these solutions defines an equilibrium conditional distribution in the market. Notice that

$$f''(y) = -(2y + k)^{-3/2} < 0, \tag{3.6}$$

as required by the second order condition (3.3).

Given $f(y)$, the individual optimizes by setting

$$(2y + k)^{-1/2} = \frac{1}{n}, \tag{3.7}$$

or

$$y(n) = \frac{n^2 - k}{2}. \tag{3.8}$$

The income net of signaling costs which results is

$$c(n) = \frac{n}{2} + \frac{k}{2n}. \tag{3.9}$$

It follows that

$$f(y(n)) = \left[2\left(\frac{n^2 - k}{2}\right) + k \right]^{1/2} = n, \tag{3.10}$$

as required in an equilibrium.

Lowering k, the arbitrary constant, increases the amount of education purchased at given levels of n, and reduces the income net of signaling. Notice also that, in this example, reductions in k damage the people with lower levels of n most, as measured by the absolute change in income net of signaling. In the discrete model, only high productivity types were hurt by upward shifts in $\bar{y}$.

I hope the example suggests that multiple equilibria are the rule rather than the exceptional case. The matter is pursued in greater detail in the appendices.

4 Model 3: Education and Race— The Informational Impact of Indices

In the education signaling model, other observable characteristics were ignored. In that model, education was a signal. In this chapter and the next, the informational impact of indices is considered. The reader will recall that an index is an unalterably observable characteristic. For concreteness, race is taken as the example. But just as education can stand for any set of observable alterable characteristics in the first model, race can stand for observable unalterable ones here. The reader may wish to think in terms of sex, nationality, size, or in terms of criminal or police records and service records. The latter is potentially public information about a person's history and is, of course, unalterable when viewed retrospectively from the present.

Model 3a: Lower Equilibrium Traps and Multiple Equilibria

Let us assume that there are two groups, blacks and whites, hereafter referred to as W and B. Within each group, the distribution of productive capabilities and the incidence of signaling costs are the same. Thus, within B, the proportion of people with productivity one and signaling (education) costs of y is q_1. The remainder have productivity two and signaling costs $y/2$.

The same is true for group W. The assumptions are summarized in Table 4.1.

Table 4.1. Data of the Model

Race	Productivity	Education costs	Proportion within group	Proportion of total population
W	1	y	q_1	$q_1(1 - b)$
W	2	$y/2$	$1 - q_1$	$(1 - q_1)(1 - b)$
B	1	y	q_1	$q_1 b$
B	2	$y/2$	$1 - q_1$	$(1 - q_1)b$

Here, b is the proportion of blacks in the overall population of job applicants.

Given the assumptions, the central question is, "How could race have an informational impact on the market?" I argue that indices do have a potential impact.

Under the stated assumptions, the conditional probability that a person drawn at random from the population has a productivity of two, given that he is black (or white), is the same as the unconditional probability that his productivity is two. Race and productivity are uncorrelated in the population. Therefore, *by itself,* race could never tell the employer anything about productivity.

This suggests the conclusion that if race is to have any informational impact, it must be through its interaction with the educational signaling game. But here again there is a puzzling symmetry. Under the assumptions, blacks and whites of equal productivity have the same signaling (education) costs. It is a general maxim in economics that people with the same preferences and opportunity sets will make similar decisions and end up in similar situations. People maximize their incomes net of signaling costs, so that their preferences are the same. And since signaling costs are the same, it would appear that their opportunity sets are the same. Hence, again, one is led to the conclusion that race can have no informational impact. But the conclusion is wrong, for an interesting reason.

The opportunity sets of blacks and whites of comparable productivity are *not* necessarily the same. To see this, let us step back to the simple educational signaling model. There are externalities in that model. One person's signaling strategy or decision affects the market data obtained by the employer, which in turn affects the employer's conditional probabilities. These determine the wages offered to various levels of education, and hence of rates of return on education for the next group in the job market. The same mechanism applies here, with a notable modification. If employers' distributions are conditional on race as well as education, then the external impact of a white's signaling decision is felt only by other whites. The same holds for blacks.

If, at some point in time, blacks and whites are not investing in education in the same ways, then the returns to education for blacks and whites will be different in the next round. In short, their opportunity sets differ. It remains to demonstrate rigorously that this sort of situation can persist in an equilibrium. The important point, however, is that there are externalities implicit in the fact that an individual is treated as the average member of the group of people who look the same and that, as a result, and in spite of an apparent sameness, the opportunity sets facing two or more groups which are visibly distinguishable may in fact be different.

The employer now has two potential signals to consider: education and race. At the start, he does not know whether either education or race will be correlated with productivity. Uninformative potential signals are naturally discarded in the course of reaching an equilibrium. As before, it is necessary to guess at an equilibrium form for the employer's expectations, and then verify that these beliefs can be self-confirming via the market informational feedback mechanisms. Try beliefs of the following form.

If W and $y < \bar{y}_W$, productivity = 1 with probability 1
If W and $y \gtreqless \bar{y}_W$, productivity = 2 with probability 1
If B and $y < \bar{y}_B$, productivity = 1 with probability 1
If B and $y \gtreqless \bar{y}_B$, productivity = 2 with probability 1.

34 Market Signaling

These lead to offered wage schedules $W_W(y)$ and $W_B(y)$ as shown in Figure 4.1.

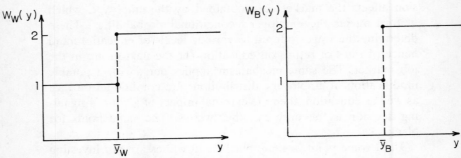

Figure 4.1. Offered Wages to W and B

Because groups W and B are distinguishable to the employer, their offered wages are not connected at the level of employer expectations. The reasoning used in the straightforward educational signaling model, applied here, yields the equilibrium conditions on $\bar{y}_W$ and $\bar{y}_B$:

$$1 < \bar{y}_W < 2,$$

and

$$1 < \bar{y}_B < 2.$$

No mathematical condition connects $\bar{y}_W$ and $\bar{y}_B$, as a result of the equilibrium analysis.[1] The equilibria are depicted in Figure 4.2.

Essentially, we simply have the educational signaling model reiterated. Because race is observable, the employer can make

1. In our simple models, an individual's marginal product does not depend upon the inputs of the same and other factors. If it did, then the actual marginal products of whites and blacks would not be independent of the number of people employed from each group. But the independence at the level of signaling would continue to hold. For a model with nonconstant marginal products, see Appendix D.

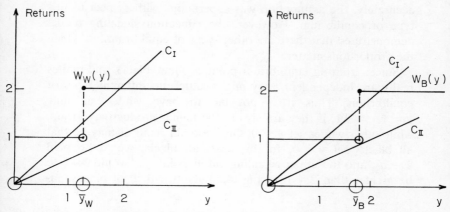

Figure 4.2. Market Equilibrium with Race as an Index

his conditional probability assessments depend upon race as well as education. This has the effect of making signaling interdependencies between two groups, W and B, totally nonexistent. They settle into signaling equilibrium configurations in the market independently of each other. But in the first model, there was not one equilibrium, there were many. Therefore there is at least the logical possibility that whites and blacks will settle into *different* stable signaling equilibria in the market, and stay there.

As noted earlier, the signaling equilibria are not equivalent, from the point of view of social welfare. The higher that $\bar{y}_W$ (or $\bar{y}_B$) is, the worse off is the relevant group or, more accurately, the high-productivity portion of the group. One example of an asymmetrical equilibrium would be given by $\bar{y}_W = 1.1$, and $\bar{y}_B = 1.9$. In this case, high-productivity blacks have to spend more on education and have less left over to consume, in order to convince the employer that they are in the high-productivity group.

Notice that the proportions of high- and low-productivity people in each group do not affect the signaling equilibrium in the market. Hence, the initial assumption that the groups were identical with respect to the distribution of productive characteristics and the incidence of signaling costs was superfluous. More accurately, the assumption was superfluous with respect to this type of equilibrium. However, the education signaling model demonstrated that there are other types of equilibrium, in which the proportions matter.

Since, from an equilibrium point of view, blacks and whites really are independent, they might settle into different types of equilibrium. Thus it is possible to have whites signaling $y = \bar{y}_W = 1.1$, if they are also in the higher-productivity group, while other whites set $y = 0$. On the other hand, it may be that all blacks set $y = 0$. In this case, all blacks would be paid $2 - q_1$, and the upper signaling cutoff point, $\bar{y}_B$, would have to be greater than $2q_1$ (see Fig. 4.3). Notice that all blacks, in-

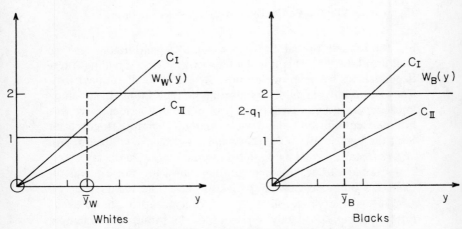

Figure 4.3. Another Equilibrium Configuration in the Market

cluding low-productivity blacks, would be paid more than low-productivity whites in this situation. High-productivity blacks would, of course, be hurt in terms of wages received. It is conceivable, however, that returns net of signaling would be higher for blacks with productivity of two. In other words, it is possible that

$$2 - q_1 > 2 - \bar{y}_W/2.$$

This will occur when

$$2q_1 < \bar{y}_W.$$

Looking at this situation from outside, one might conclude that blacks receive lower wages than some whites because of a lack of education which keeps their productivity down. One might then go looking outside the job market for the explanation for the lack of education. In this model, the analysis just suggested would be wrong. The source of the signaling and wage differentials is in the informational structure of the market itself. The impacts of differential signaling costs are considered in the next chapter.

Because of the independence of the two groups, B and W, at the level of signaling, one can generate many different possible equilibrium configurations by taking any of the equilibria in model 2 and assigning it to W, and then taking any other model 2 equilibrium and assigning it to B. However, an exhaustive listing of the possibilities seems pointless at this stage.

Quite apart from other possible impacts of indices upon the performance of the job market, the interaction of signals and indices creates the possibility of arbitrary differences in the equilibrium signaling configurations of two or more distinct groups. Some of them may be at a disadvantage relative to others. Subsets of one may be at a disadvantage relative to comparable subsets of the others. Since the mechanism which generates the equilibrium is a feedback loop, one might, following Myrdal and others, wish to refer to the situation of the disadvantaged group as a vicious cycle, albeit an informationally based one. Alternatively, one can refer to the situation of the disadvantaged group as a lower-level equilibrium trap, which conveys the notion of a situation that, once achieved, persists for reasons that are endogenous to the model. The multiple equilibria of the education model translate into arbitrary differences in the equilibrium configuration and status of two groups, as defined as observable, unalterable characteristics.[2]

2. In the next chapter, the effects of adopting the policy of suppressing the visibility of the index, race, in hiring process are examined.

5 Model 3b: Differential Signaling Costs

If education costs are different for groups W and B, they will affect the signaling equilibrium and the informational structure of the market. The unprejudiced employer will tend, in making his probabilistic assessments, to compensate for the higher signaling costs facing one group. He will do this automatically in interpreting past market data. He need not be aware that education costs more for B than for W.

To see what outcomes may occur, consider the modification of model 3a in Table 5.1.

Table 5.1. Data of the Differential Signaling Cost Model

Race	Productivity	Education costs	Proportion of own group
W	1	y	q_1
W	2	$y/2$	$1 - q_1$
B	1	$2y$	q_1
B	2	y	$1 - q_1$

As compared with model 3, the signaling costs facing blacks have simply been raised. As before, employers' beliefs are based on critical levels $\bar{y}_W$ and $\bar{y}_B$. If $y < \bar{y}_B$ (or $\bar{y}_W$), the assumed productivity is one. Otherwise, productivity is taken to be two.

The offered wage schedules and equilibrium choices are shown in Figure 5.1.

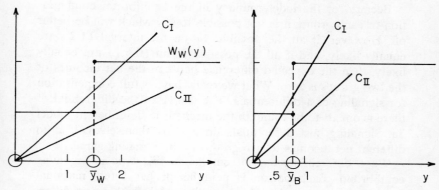

Figure 5.1. Equilibrium in the Market

The conditions on $\bar{y}_W$ and $\bar{y}_B$ which lead to an equilibrium are

$$1 < \bar{y}_W < 2,$$

as before, but

$$0.5 < \bar{y}_B < 1.$$

The allowable interval for $\bar{y}_B$ is shifted down.

	Race	
	White	Black
one	1 1	1 1
two	2 $2-\bar{y}_W/2$	2 $2-\bar{y}_B$

Productivity

Figure 5.2. Wages and Returns Net of Signaling

In Figure 5.2 and subsequent diagrams like it, wage is in the upper left, return net of education costs in the lower right of each box.

Because of the indeterminacy in the equilibrium configuration of each group, it is not possible to say which will be better off. However, if all the possible $\bar{y}_W$ on the interval $(1,2)$ are equally likely, and if all the possible $\bar{y}_B$ on $(0.5,1)$ are equally likely, then the expected difference between the net incomes of the two groups is zero. What we really have is full compensation for signaling cost differentials. The source of the differential, if there is one, is to be found in the mechanism described in model 3a. Signaling cost differentials do not, by themselves, lead to different net incomes to two groups in the signaling game.

Wage differentials do not emerge in this type of signaling equilibrium. Each person is paid his or her actual marginal product. However, there are equilibria in which wage differentials can be observed. The set of employer beliefs which might generate them is as follows.

If W and $y < \bar{y}_W$, productivity $= 1$ with probability 1
If W and $y \gtrless \bar{y}_W$, productivity $= 2$ with probability 1
If B and $y < \bar{y}_B$, productivity $= 1$ with probability q_1
$\qquad\qquad\qquad\qquad\qquad\;\; = 2$ with probability $1 - q_1$
If B and $y \gtrless \bar{y}_B$, productivity $= 2$ with probability 1.

These beliefs will be confirmed if whites follow the same pattern as above while all blacks set $y = 0$. The required conditions on $\bar{y}_W$ and $\bar{y}_B$ for this to occur are

$$1 < \bar{y}_W < 2,$$

as before, but

$$\bar{y}_B > q_1.$$

The wages and returns net of signaling in this example are shown in Figure 5.3.

Because of the high signaling costs facing blacks, $\bar{y}_B$ does not have to be very high in order to make it rational for even the high-productivity black to select the lower level of education. When we examined this case under model 3a, where there were no cost differentials, we found the condition on $\bar{y}_B$ to be

$$\bar{y}_B > 2q_1.$$

Race

		White	Black
Productivity	one	1 1	$2-q_1$ $2-q_1$
	two	2 $2-\bar{y}_W/2$	$2-q_1$ $2-q_1$

Figure 5.3. Wages and Returns Net of Signaling

Here $\bar{y}_B$ need be only half as large to produce the asymmetrical signaling patterns over the two groups, W and B. Moreover, the effect is reinforced because once a situation in which no one is investing in education obtains, the wages of those setting $y = 0$ (i.e., everyone) rise from $W = 1$ to $W = 2 - q_1$.

In the situation in which both groups are investing in education, the educational prerequisite $\bar{y}$ is lower for the group with the high signaling costs. Viewed naively or from the outside, this might look like reverse discrimination. But it is not, provided the standard is equal treatment in terms of wages of people with equal productive capabilities. In fact, nondiscrimination at the level of rewarding productive capability implies discrimination at the level of signals. Conversely, failure to discriminate at the level of signals implies discrimination at the level of salaries and productive capabilities.

Suppressing Potential Indices

A signaling mechanism can allow two or more groups, as defined by observable unalterable characteristics, to settle into different signaling equilibria. Systematic differences in signaling costs over two or more groups, similarly defined, have signaling impacts. If an index is the basis of unequal treatment of groups, it is natural to think in terms of suppressing the index by finding ways to make it difficult or impossible for the employer to observe it. For example, in a slightly different context, most colleges and universities at least nominally deny themselves access to information on race and religion.

The problem is not confined to race. Sex is an index which may provide the basis for an informationally based asymmetry in the signaling equilibrium of men and women in different classes of work. Similarly, there are important policy decisions to be made concerning police records, arrests, convictions, medical and health information, service records, past political affiliations, and so on. All of these, if made easily accessible to employers, are indices with the potential impacts attributed to race in the last two models.

There are, of course, problems with suppressing indices. Race and sex can be suppressed only by eliminating face-to-face contact upon which employers may currently rely in making hiring decisions. On the other hand, this is not a problem with criminal records. The technology of controlling indices is a large subject and is dealt with only briefly later. The point I wish to make here concerns the source of unequal treatment and the equilibrium effects of suppressing indices.

Proposition: If the source of the unequal treatment of two groups is an arbitrary difference in the equilibrium situation of two groups who are otherwise similarly situated with respect to productive capabilities and signaling costs, then suppressing the index which defines the groups will eliminate the unequal treatment. On the other hand, if the source is differences in signaling costs, then suppressing the index will produce wage discrimination and may hurt the high-signaling-cost group.

The proposition can be illustrated with a simple example. The data are given in Table 5.2.

Table 5.2. Data of the Model

Race	Productivity	Education costs	Proportion in group	Proportion in population
W	1	y	q_1	$q_1(1-b)$
W	2	$y/2$	$1-q_1$	$(1-q_1)(1-b)$
B	1	$2y$	q_1	$q_1 b$
B	2	y	$1-q_1$	$(1-q_1)b$

In an equilibrium situation, if all of B and the lower productivity group within W set $y = 0$, the employer's beliefs will take the following form.

If $y < \bar{y}$, productivity = 1 with probability r,
    productivity = 2 with probability $1 - r$,
If $y \gtrless \bar{y}$, productivity = 2 with probability 1.

(Note that y is the only signal, since the index has been suppressed.) The required value for r is given by

$$r = \frac{1}{1 + b\dfrac{(1 - q_1)}{q_1}}.$$

For concreteness, let us assume that $b = 0.1$ and $q_1 = .375$. It follows that $r = 6/7$.

Given the expectations, the offered wage schedule is

$$W(y) = 8/7 \quad \text{if} \quad y < \bar{y},$$
$$W(y) = 2 \quad\quad \text{if} \quad y \gtrless \bar{y}.$$

It is depicted in Figure 5.4.

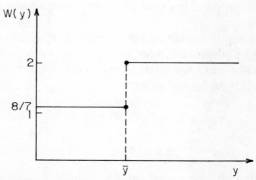

Figure 5.4. Offered Wages to Education

It is necessary to verify that all groups and subgroups make the requisite choices.

1. W and productivity = 1: selects $y = 0$ provided that

$$8/7 > 2 - \bar{y}.$$

2. W and productivity = 2: selects $y = \bar{y}$ provided that

$$2 - \bar{y}/2 > 8/7.$$

3. B and productivity = 1: selects $y = 0$ provided that

$$8/7 > 2 - 2\bar{y}.$$

4. B and productivity = 2: selects $y = 0$ provided that

$$8/7 > 2 - \bar{y}.$$

Notice that conditions 1 and 4 are the same. These two groups will always make the same signaling decisions in equilibrium, because (a) their education costs are the same, and (b) since they can't be distinguished, the wage schedules they face are the same. This assertion enjoys the status of a perfectly general theorem in market signaling games of this type.

The market will be in an equilibrium provided that

$$6/7 < \bar{y} < 12/7.$$

The equilibrium payoffs to the two groups are shown in Figure 5.5.

The next step is to compare the results here with those found in the case in which the index was not suppressed. For reference, the outcome of the latter is exhibited in Figure 5.6. The constraints on $\bar{y}_W$ and $\bar{y}_B$ were

$$1 < \bar{y}_W < 2,$$

and

$$0.5 < \bar{y}_B < 1.$$

The following differences are worthy of note.

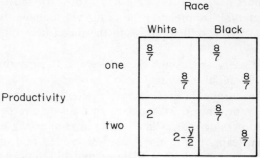

Figure 5.5. Wages and Net Incomes

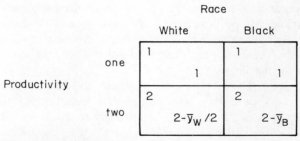

Figure 5.6. Equilibrium Wages and Net Incomes

1. The wages of all people with productivity one are raised from 1 to 8/7.

2. Wages of high-productivity whites are the same at two.

3. Wages of high-productivity blacks fall from 2 to 8/7. Hence wage discrimination is introduced.

4. All low-productivity people have higher net incomes by 1/7.

5. The sign of the change of the net income of high-productivity whites is indeterminate. If $\bar{y} = \bar{y}_W$, this group is better off when the index is suppressed. Note that the allowable range for $\bar{y}$ is $(6/7, 12/7)$, while the allowable range for $\bar{y}_W$ was $(1,2)$. Hence, we might expect $\bar{y} < \bar{y}_W$.

6. The net income of high-productivity blacks goes from $2 - \bar{y}_B$ to 8/7. The allowable range for $\bar{y}_B$ was $(0.5,1)$. This

group is hurt if $\bar{y}_B$ was less than $6/7$. Thus, for most of the allowable interval, suppressing the index will damage this group. Only if $\bar{y}_B > 6/7$, will suppressing the index help high-productivity blacks.

Without carrying through the analysis, it is clear that if there are no differential signaling costs, suppressing the index will eliminate arbitrary differences in the equilibrium configuration of the relevant groups, without any of the side effects discussed above. Suppressing indices is effective in eliminating lower-level equilibrium traps, but it may have unintended and undesirable consequences when there are systematic differences in education (or other signaling) costs in the society. These differences arise from discrimination or other factors exogenous to the labor market, and presumably that is where the problem should be attacked. My purpose here is not to dispose of the issue (and I certainly have not), but rather to draw attention to the consequences of various strategies conditional upon the underlying data of the market signaling game.

One point, however, is clear. If there are differences in signaling costs (and this principle applies well beyond the job market), it is not possible simultaneously to avoid discriminating at the levels of both signals and underlying capabilities. To fail to discriminate with respect to the former is to discriminate with respect to the latter. Suppressing indices, then, is a risky strategy at best, although one might still opt for it to prevent prejudice from having any effect on the market.

The inadequacy of the simple policy of suppressing a signal is implicitly recognized by many admissions boards who, while retaining the principle of not acknowledging race or other similar factors in their decisions, in fact, in the interests of fairness, find it desirable and necessary to compensate for the extreme educational disadvantages which afflict portions of many minorities in the precollege period. In general, standing upon the principle of color blindness may be unsatisfactory, given that various kinds of ability must be estimated indirectly from limited information in the form of signals such as educational performance and indices like tests, and that these signals mean different things for different groups as a result of discrimination and other factors outside the particular market under consideration.

6 Model 4: Randomness in Signaling Costs

In the education signaling in model 2, it was assumed that education costs were perfectly negatively correlated with productivity. In the context of that model, the effect of the assumption was to make y the basis for a perfect point prediction of productivity, at least in some market equilibrium configurations. It is desirable to relax that somewhat unrealistic assumption and to determine the effects on the signaling equilibrium. Basically, the pattern of signaling observed in the earlier model continues to hold, with some interesting modifications.

Signaling costs are intended to include a variety of costs incurred in undertaking the signaling activity. Some of these are subjective. One individual may find the process of acquiring an education extremely distasteful, while another of comparable ability thoroughly enjoys it. Moreover, we can extend the interpretation of "signaling costs" to include differences in tastes for particular jobs. These types of subjective factors, because they are unobservable to the employer, will tend to produce variations in the signaling behavior of individuals of equal productive potential. These variations are referred to as random if they are imperfectly correlated with anything which the employer can observe.

There is a third possible source of randomness in signaling costs. There may be nonsubjective sources of differential signaling costs which the employer observes only with difficulty. A possible example is parents' income. The individual whose family is poor will often face higher real costs of acquiring an education than the more well-to-do offspring. Now, parents' income is not directly observable. It might occur to the employer to ask about it, but then it is relatively easy for the sophisticated job applicant to understate his parents' income. Therefore, even if it occurs to the employer to ask about family income (not a common practice, by the way), he will not receive reliable reports and hence the "information" will be of relatively little value.

Randomness in signaling costs may arise from subjective factors relating to the signaling activity or the job, and from unobservable or disguisable real differences in the signaling costs of applicants. Whatever the source, the effect is to produce random variations in the productive capabilities of individuals who exhibit the same signals and hence look the same to the employer at the time he hires them. A modification of model 2 will serve as an example.

Assume that the high-productivity group is divided into two subgroups, denoted II.a and II.b. The signaling cost function for Group II.a is $y/2$ as before. The signaling costs for Group II.b, however, are raised to y and hence are the same as those of Group I (see Table 6.1).

Table 6.1. Data of the Market

Group	Productivity	Education costs	Proportion of the population
I	1	y	1/3
II.a	2	$y/2$	1/3
II.b	2	y	1/3

For concreteness the reader may think of Group II.b as the high-productivity group with high signaling costs resulting from having poor parents.

Groups I and II.b will always behave in the same way in a signaling equilibrium. They are indistinguishable and have the same signaling costs. This means that they will always be commingled by the employer in an equilibrium. No educational signaling mechanism will distinguish them.

It is likely that there are equilibrium employer-beliefs of the following form.

If $y < \bar{y}$, productivity = 1 with probability 1/2,
productivity = 2 with probability 1/2,
If $y \gtrless \bar{y}$, productivity = 2 with probability 1.

The offered wage schedule is the step function depicted in Figure 6.1.

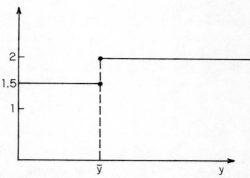

Figure 6.1. Offered Wages to Education

Beliefs are confirmed by experience in the market, if Groups I and II.b set $y = 0$, and Group II.a sets $y = \bar{y}$. The conditions are

$$1.5 > 2 - \bar{y},$$

and

$$2 - \frac{\bar{y}}{2} > 1.5.$$

Therefore, the allowable range for $\bar{y}$ is

$$0.5 < \bar{y} < 1.$$

Equilibrium outcomes are represented in Figure 6.2 and Table 6.2.

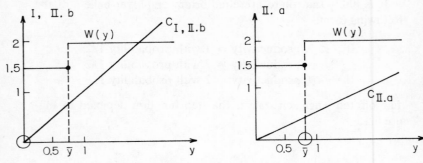

Figure 6.2. Optimal Choices of Education in the Equilibrium

Table 6.2. Wages and Net Income

	Group I	Group II.b	Group II.a
Wages	1.5	1.5	2
Net Income	1.5	1.5	$2 - \bar{y}/2$

The basic pattern of the signaling equilibrium is much like those already observed. There is a continuum of equilibria. Increases in $\bar{y}$ within the interval $(0.5, 1)$ hurt II.a and help no one. Group II.b receives wages which are lower than productivity. Group I has wages which exceed productive capability. Its members are the principal beneficiaries of the fact that education costs for II.b are too high to allow them to distinguish themselves. Of course, with a slight modification, marginal product could be allowed to vary with the number employed. If this were done, then Group II.a benefits, since the high costs facing Group II.b effectively eliminate competition from the members of that group.

The employer does not receive perfect information anymore. In this example, when $y = 0$, hiring is purchasing a genuine lottery. If the employer were risk-averse (up to this point he has been risk-neutral), that would affect his behavior.[1] Randomness

---

1. For a discussion of the effects of employer risk-aversion, see Appendix C.

in signaling costs does not necessarily render education useless as a signal. In fact, considerable randomness is compatible with having an effective signal, provided only that there remains a component of signaling costs which varies systematically with productive capability.

Randomness (and here randomness always means randomness as viewed from the perspective of the employer) has two different types of origin. One source is essentially subjective and a matter of taste. And one can wonder whether a distaste for education leading to higher signaling costs of presenting a favorable image in the market is an appropriate component in a market screening mechanism. The second source is real resource cost differences or opportunity cost differences in acquiring an education. Such differences are relevant if their source is effectively hidden from the employer. When it is, the screening mechanism is discriminatory. High-productivity, high-signaling-cost people will always invest in ways which are similar to lower-productivity and lower-signaling-cost people. As a result, they will look the same to the employer and therefore receive the same salaries. The former group will be, in a sense, subsidizing the latter. It does so by raising the average productivity of people using a certain signal.

A Continuous Model of Randomness in Signaling Costs

In discussing educational signaling, we examined a continuous version of the market equilibrium model. Multiple equilibria appeared in that model, and the structure of the equilibrium was similar to that found in the discrete cases. Here, the discrete model with randomness is generalized to a continuous case.

Assumptions and Notation

1. Productivity, denoted by n, is a random variable.
2. Educational signaling costs are θy where θ is a random variable.

3. The joint distribution of n and θ in the population is $q(n,\theta)$. Since n and θ are unalterable attributes, this distribution is well defined.

4. The expected value of n given y is denoted by $W(y)$. It is the offered wage schedule.

The problem is that of finding an equilibrium set of conditional probabilities, or, alternatively, an equilibrium schedule, $W(y)$. Assume $W(y)$ is given. An individual for whom y units of education cost θy dollars will optimally select his level of education by setting

$$W'(y) = \theta. \tag{6.1}$$

The second order condition is

$$W''(y) < 0. \tag{6.2}$$

Once these optimizing decisions are made, we can use the joint distribution $q(n,\theta)$ to find the new joint distribution of n and y, by substituting for θ. Let $p_W(n,y)$ be the new joint distribution of n and y. Applying the change of variable technique for fixed n, we find that

$$p_W(n,y) = q(n,W'(y))|W''(y)|. \tag{6.3}$$

Using the new joint distribution of n and y, we compute the expected value of n given y to be

$$E(n|y) = \frac{\int n p_W(n,y)\,dn}{\int p_W(n,y)\,dn}. \tag{6.4}$$

In equilibrium, this expected value must equal $W(y)$. Thus, the equilibrium is defined by the relation

$$\frac{\int n q(n,W'(y))\,dn}{\int q(n,W'(y))\,dn} = W(y). \tag{6.5}$$

As before, this is a first order differential equation in $W(y)$ and has a solution which consists of a one-parameter family of curves. These are the multiple equilibria in the random model.

We can derive the equilibrium class of schedules $W(y)$ in a specific case by assuming that $q(n,\theta)$ is a bivariate normal density function. Actually, since we do not want n or θ to be negative, we assume that $q(n,\theta)$ is very close to normal and treat it as if it were. Let

$$\bar{n} = \text{the mean of } n$$
$$\bar{\theta} = \text{the mean of } \theta$$
$$\sigma_n^2 = \text{the variance of } n$$
$$\sigma_\theta^2 = \text{the variance of } \theta$$
$$\sigma_{n\theta} = \text{the covariance of } n \text{ and } \theta.$$

For effective signaling to take place, we assume $\sigma_{n\theta} < 0$. In the nonrandom case $\theta = 1/n$, and the negative correlation of n and signaling costs was perfect.

These assumptions, in conjunction with a well-known fact about bivariate normal distributions, yield the equilibrium condition[2] yield

$$\bar{n} + \frac{\sigma_{\theta n}}{\sigma_\theta^2}(W'(y) - \bar{\theta}) = W(y), \qquad (6.6)$$

or

$$W'(y) - \frac{\sigma_\theta^2}{\sigma_{\theta n}}W(y) = \bar{\theta} - \bar{n}\frac{\sigma_\theta^2}{\sigma_{\theta n}}. \qquad (6.7)$$

Let $A = -\dfrac{\sigma_\theta^2}{\sigma_{\theta n}}$ and $B = \bar{\theta} - \bar{n}\dfrac{\sigma_\theta^2}{\sigma_{\theta n}}$. It follows that $A > 0, B > 0$, and

$$W'(y) + AW(y) = B. \qquad (6.8)$$

2. The fact we need here is that the conditional distribution of n given θ (or equivalently $W'(y)$) is normal with mean

$$\bar{n} + \frac{\sigma_{\theta n}}{\sigma_\theta^2}(\theta - \bar{\theta}),$$

and variance

$$\theta_n^2 - \frac{\sigma_\theta^2 n}{\sigma_\theta^2}.$$

The solution to (6.8) is

$$W(y) = \frac{B}{A} - ke^{-Ay}, \qquad (6.9)$$

where k is an arbitrary constant. To ensure that $W(y)$ is concave, we must stipulate that $k > 0$. This is the family of equilibrium offered-wage schedules in the model. Notice that as $\sigma_{\theta n}$ approaches zero from below, $A \to +\infty$, $B \to \bar{n}$ and $W(y) \to \bar{n}$, the unconditional mean of n. This is surely what one would expect.

Working backward, the equilibrium conditional distribution of n given y is found to be normal with mean

$$\bar{n} + \frac{\sigma_{n\theta}}{\sigma_\theta{}^2} (W'(y) - \bar{\theta}), \qquad (6.10)$$

and variance,

$$\sigma_n{}^2 - \frac{\sigma_{\theta n}{}^2}{\sigma_\theta{}^2}. \qquad (6.11)$$

Notice that the variance does not depend on y in this case. Again as $\sigma_{\theta n} \to 0$ the mean and variance approach $\bar{n}$ and $\sigma_n{}^2$ respectively, as one would expect.

It is interesting to determine which individuals will be paid more than their marginal products. Consider an individual characterized by the pair (n,θ). His wage is determined entirely by θ. Given $W(y)$, he optimally selects y by setting

$$kAe^{-Ay} = \theta, \qquad (6.12)$$

or

$$y(\theta) = -\frac{1}{A} \log \left(\frac{\theta}{kA} \right). \qquad (6.13)$$

As a result, he receives the wage

$$W(y(\theta)) = \frac{\bar{\theta} - \theta}{A} + \bar{n}. \qquad (6.14)$$

Hence, his wage is greater than his marginal product, provided that

$$\frac{\bar{\theta} - \theta}{A} + \bar{n} > n. \qquad (6.15)$$

The regions in which wages exceed or fall short of productivity are shown in Figure 6.3.

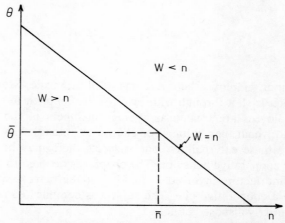

Figure 6.3. Relation of Wages to Productivity in the Random Costs Case

7 Cooperative Behavior

Throughout, employee behavior has been atomistic. Moreover, the market is shot through with externalities, implicit in the fact that employees are treated as average members of the visible groups to which they belong (or choose to belong). Given that there are these externalities, one suspects there may be incentives for cooperative behavior. The chapter is devoted to considering some factors involved in looking at the market signaling game as a cooperative one. The subject is complicated and will not be entirely disposed of here.

Deliberate collective action to affect the informational structure of the market presupposes that someone is aware that signaling is actually occurring. While one may wish to make this supposition, there is nothing in the atomistic model which guarantees that either employees or employers are aware that education is a signal. This is especially true of the employee who only has to worry about the private return to education. And even if he thinks of education as a signal, his optimal investment in education, given the wage schedule, will be the same.

Employers are more likely to know that education is only one factor in determining productivity and that the return to education is higher than its direct contribution to productivity. This awareness would be hard to avoid in the case where signaling costs have a random component, so that productivity is only imperfectly correlated with productivity (see model 4).

The employer, however, will be able to exploit his knowledge only in special circumstances. He must have a relatively captive labor force. Otherwise, raising education requirements will cause an exodus of potential employees to other markets. He must also be able to appropriate some of the increases in individual productivity which result from higher levels of investment in education.

If employees were aware of signaling, what kinds of coalitions might form to affect the informational structure of the market, and under what circumstances? In the atomistic models, there are Pareto inferior market equilibria.

For example, in model 2 with $\bar{y} = 1.7$, any reduction in $\bar{y}$ helps high-productivity types while hurting neither employer nor lower-productivity employees. Translated into the language of cooperative game theory, many signaling equilibria are blocked by the coalition of everyone. This, of course, abstracts from the costs of organizing the blocking coalition, which may be the operative factor in preventing the blocking move from taking place.

Carrying the analysis one step further, note that any signaling at all uses resources in a way which produces no social product. Therefore, any signaling equilibrium is blocked by the coalition of everyone. Thus all the signaling equilibria we have observed are ruled out in the fully cooperative game. And they are ruled out by virtue of being blocked by the coalition of everyone.

Now the interesting question arises as to what the outcome of the cooperative game will be, if it is not one of the signaling equilibria previously observed. This turns out to be a quite complicated question. It proves useful to investigate the matter under a variety of alternative assumptions. The complexity results from the fact that education served an informational function in the atomistic model. The question then is what, if anything, takes the place of the education signal in the cooperative game.

Having eliminated educational signaling, we may temporarily drop back to the no-signaling model where everyone receives the average productivity in the population, $2 - q_1$. Is this outcome stable? The group which may have an incentive to upset it is the higher-productivity group. If this group can find a way to (a) identify its members and (b) certify them, then it can collect its actual marginal product of 2, instead of the average of $2 - q_1$ over the whole population. Whether it is worth it depends upon the costs of identification and certification.

Let us assume that to identify the higher-productivity types, it is necessary to administer a test to everyone in the relevant population. The cost is c units per person. Infallible certification is assumed to be costless. The return to the group with certification is

$$2(1 - q_1)p - cp,$$

where p is the total population. Without certification, the return is

$$(2 - q_1)(1 - q_1)p.$$

Hence it is easily verified that it is rational to test everyone and to certify the qualified, provided that

$$c < 2q_1(1-q_1).$$

The maximum tolerable per-person testing cost is $\frac{1}{4}$ and occurs when $q_1 = \frac{1}{2}$.

A special case occurs when $c = 0$, that is, when members of Group II can costlessly identify each other. In this case, they will always certify their members. When this happens, the outcome is the perfectly competitive equilibrium in a hypothetical world of perfect information. This is a perfectly general theorem. If all productively relevant groupings can costlessly identify and certify their members, the cooperative game has a unique point in the core, and it is the competitive equilibrium in a world of perfect information. The proof is given in Appendix I.

Testing and certifying is nothing more nor less than self-licensing. It need not take the bald form of testing everyone. There may be an educational prerequisite for taking the test. In this way, educational signaling would come back into the system through the back door. In general, testing would be administered by a group representing the higher-productivity types.

There is also the interesting question who bears the cost of the screening. The argument above assumed the higher-productivity group absorbs the cost. If individuals are asked to bear the cost, some may select themselves out, anticipating being screened out anyway. This would reduce the screening costs and make self-licensing more viable. Cost sharing is also a possible mixed case.

If the coalition of everyone *does not* form to block all signaling, then an organization representing higher-productivity people may form to lower the educational prerequisite, $\bar{y}$. (Of course, they wouldn't want it lowered too much, for then lower-productivity types would set $y = \bar{y}$ and confuse the signaling system.) Educational signaling would persist, but the market equilibrium would be more advantageous to the high-productivity types. This kind of collective action simply amounts to shifting a signaling equilibrium to a Pareto superior one.

It is also possible to find the reverse taking place. If the market is in a no-signaling equilibrium with everyone setting $y = 0$, representatives of Group II might campaign for the installment of an educational requirement $\bar{y}$, to serve as a way for its members to distinguish themselves in the market. Such a strategy is rational provided q_1, the proportion of lower-productivity people, exceeds the ratio of the marginal signaling costs, a_2/a_1 (see model 2).

If $\bar{y}$, the educational prerequisite, is too high, and an organization representing Group II cannot manage to lower it, they may resort to testing and self-licensing as discussed above. If c is the unit cost of testing, it is easily verified that the strategy is rational, provided that

$$c < \frac{\bar{y}}{2}(1 - q_1).$$

If individuals bear the burden of the test, then the condition above becomes simply

$$c < \frac{\bar{y}}{2}.$$

In the latter case, it is quite likely that self-screening will take place. Unfortunately, mistakes will be made. Some who should have tried will not, while others who try will fail.

One might ask why the employer does not administer the test himself. One possible answer is that he need not, since education is currently serving the informational function quite well. Another is that the cost of administering the test may be much higher for the employer than for the group representing potential employees.

There are many examples of coalitions and effective organized screening. Both doctors and lawyers screen their own. They use previous education as a preliminary screen and then more education as the test. The education is also productive. In both cases costs are shared, but a large part of the testing cost is borne by the applicant for certification. The reason doctors and lawyers self-screen is that they provide a service, quality control, for which they are handsomely rewarded. In addition, the costs of quality screening by their employers, the public, would be gigantic as compared with the self-screening costs.

The internal labor market as described by Doeringer and Piore is another example of self-screening.[1] The employer hands over the promotion process to the union organization in return for a certain amount of quality control. He abstains from the signaling game altogether. The union is an interesting example of an organization which exists for other purposes and then takes on a signaling function. The signaling function by itself would probably not justify the costs of maintaining the organization.

Employment agencies can and do take over the signaling and information gathering function in some instances. Here, the atomistic signaling game is played between employees and agencies. There are economies of scale available to the agency. A candidate need be evaluated only once and then can be sent to a number of different employers. Hence agencies can often screen applicants for less than employers could.

1. Peter Doeringer and Michael Piore, *Internal Labor Markets and Manpower Analysis* (Boston: D. C. Heath, 1971).

There are other groups with a potential impact on the informational structure of job markets. People who go to the same church, belong to the same club, who served in the military together, or attended the same college belong to quasi-natural groups with potential power over the information system. They can, to some extent, certify each other. Minority groups with internal organizations which exist primarily to serve the ends of the members of the minority could also have an informational impact.

My intention here has not been to cover exhaustively the large subject of the informational impact of existing organizations, potential or actual; it is to indicate that there is, because of externalities, ample scope for cooperative behavior or collective action, and to suggest some of the forms this collective action might take. Self-testing and screening and the elimination or institution of educational or other standards are among them. Implicit in the job market signaling models is a process whereby people are sorted not only into salary levels and classes, but into different jobs as well. There remains the rather large question, which we have only touched upon here, concerning alternative societal mechanisms that perform the same function. The question is important because, in the end, its answer determines the standard by which the market mechanism is judged. Although some market equilibria can be seen to be less efficient (in the Pareto sense) than other market equilibria, and although there are potential discriminatory effects in the signaling process, the question of the best alternative institutions for performing the same job allocation function remains open.

8 Status, Income, and Consumption

Thorstein Veblen many years ago suggested that highly visible consumption is used by people as a signal of wealth and, by inference, power and status. The reasoning was relatively straightforward. Anyone who could afford high levels of conspicuous consumption must be wealthy, and this wealth must have derived from some attribute of the individual which distinguishes him or her from the rest of the society. The inference works best in a competitive society. The individual might be the hunter with the most prowess, or he might be the shrewdest and most dynamic entrepreneur. It is less adequate in societies in which there is a high probability that the individual's wealth is, in some sense, inherited. It may be that wealth is not directly inherited, but rather the opportunity to acquire it with relatively little effort (by virtue of being born into a relatively small class of people who have access to positions in which the accumulation of wealth is possible).

Abstracting from Veblen's quite sophisticated analysis of the sociology of conspicuous consumption, the point is that visible consumption goods are signals. The logic of the signaling game involved in conspicuous consumption is very similar to the structure of the job market signaling game. It is not desirable to go into status signaling in detail here, but merely to show that the models already constructed for the job market can be used to gain insights into the process. Particularly interesting is the possibility of multiple status signaling equilibria with the same kinds of welfare implications as those found in job market signaling.[1]

As a first approximation, it is assumed that status depends upon income, so that the primary problem for the household is to signal income via its consumption patterns.

One difference between the labor market models and the status signaling model is that, in the status case, everyone is similarly situated. There are not two sides to the market, and hence receivers and senders of signals are not distinct groups. The difference is especially interesting, because it turns out not to be crucial to the signaling structure of the market. Because of the symmetry of the situation, the signaling game is comparable to a coordination game, with one difference: the equilibria are not equivalent. Analogizing from two to many people, we can think of the equilibrium configurations as strategy pairs corresponding to diagonal entries in a payoff matrix, where the

Figure 8.1. A Sliding Scale of Coordination Equilibria

payoffs for each individual decline as one moves down the diagonal (see Fig. 8.1).

1. I am grateful to Richard Zeckhauser for pointing out that status is signaled by conspicuous consumption and that the effect is to distort individual consumption patterns. On reflection, the example turned out to have the logical structure of the job market case.

The off-diagonal elements are to be filled in such a way as to make each diagonal element an equilibrium. This type of problem is discussed extensively in Thomas Schelling, *The Strategy of Conflict*.

The simple status model requires the definition of three variables. One is visible consumption, denoted by c. Another is consumption which is not visible, denoted by i. Consumption in both of these areas is measured in dollars. The last variable is income, y. It is given for the individual and is distributed in the population. For ease of exposition, it is assumed that while income varies over people, utility functions do not. Utility is assumed to depend upon c and i, and also directly upon y, on the assumption that y is a proxy for status. Thus

$$u = u(c,i,y).$$

The assumption that utility functions do not vary in this model is similar to the assumption that education signaling costs vary only with productivity (see model 2, Chapter 3). As we have seen, the signaling patterns that are observable in that case persist when random variations over individuals are introduced.

Because of the absence of variation in utility functions, the equilibrium in the market, defined in terms of people's subjective beliefs concerning the relationship between c and y, will be a degenerate. That is to say, in an equilibrium, conspicuous consumption will serve as the basis of a perfect point predictor of income, much as education served as a perfect predictor of productivity in model 2.

We may deal briefly with the relationships which define an equilibrium. At a point in time, an individual will believe that the relationship between c and y is given by

$$y = h(c).$$

Using this believed fact, he will maximize his utility by selecting observable consumption levels c, keeping in mind that others' beliefs about his income will depend upon his choice of c. Formally, the problem is to

$$\max_{c} u(c, y - c, h(c)).$$

His income y is, of course, fixed.

After everyone has done this, it will turn out that the real relationship between c and y in the population is the one which emerges out of the optimizing decisions described above. People, over time, will discover this relationship by observing their own behavior and through conversations with friends, and ultimately they will revise their beliefs and adjust accordingly. Another round begins.

The process will stop when the relationship between c and y, which emerges from the optimizing decisions of individuals, is the same as the relationship which people believed when they made these decisions. In other words, as with the employer in the labor market, an equilibrium is achieved when everyone's beliefs are confirmed by subsequent experience in the market and in the society.

It is worth noting that, as in the labor market, it is necessary to assume that there is some informational feedback after the consumption decisions are made. If no such information were forthcoming, then people could not test their beliefs. It seems reasonable to assume that informational feedback through friends does occur, so that beliefs are in fact testable over time.

That is the logical structure of the model. It only remains to pursue it to discover the properties of equilibrium configurations in the market. Assuming for the moment that first-order conditions are sufficient for a maximum, the individual with income y will set

$$u_1(c, y - c, h) - u_2(c, y - c, h) + u_3(c, y - c, h)h' = 0.$$

The equilibrium condition is that

$$y = h(c).$$

Substituting for y in the optimizing condition yields

$$u_1(c, h - c, h) - u_2(c, h - c, h) + u_3(c, h - c, h)h' = 0.$$

This is the differential equation which defines the class of equilibrium functions h in the market. Because it is a differential equation, the general solution will have an arbitrary constant in it, and that arbitrary constant corresponds to the multiplicity of equilibria in this market and in the labor market. There will not be one equilibrium or even several; there will be a whole continuum of them.

It is necessary to check that the first-order condition used in finding the equilibrium in fact gave us a maximum. The second-order condition will be some expression of the form

$$D < 0.$$

Now if the equilibrium condition is differentiated with respect to c, and solved for D, one finds that

$$D = (u_{22} - u_{12} - u_{23}h')h'.$$

It is clear that $h' > 0$. Thus, D will be negative as required provided that the expression in brackets is negative. Taking u as a von Neumann-Morgenstern utility function, the condition is assured if we make the plausible assumptions that $u_{22} < 0$, while u_{12} and u_{23} are nonnegative.

To study equilibrium configurations, it is convenient to have a soluble example to deal with. Soluble examples are not easy to come by in this context, for technical reasons. But if we take

$$u(c, i, y) = c + y + \log(i),$$

some progress can be made. With this utility function, the equation defining equilibrium expectations in the market is

$$h' = \frac{1}{h - c} - 1.$$

The implicit solution for h as a function of c is given by

$$2h + \log(1 - 2h + 2c) = K - 2c,$$

where K is the expected arbitrary constant of integration.[2]

Our concern is with how individual well-being changes with shifts in the equilibrium corresponding to shifts in the parameter K. Note that if y were directly observable, so that no signaling were necessary, then the optimal level for c would be $y - 1$. On the other hand, with signaling, we must have $1 - 2h + 2c > 0$, so that $c > h - 1/2$, and c is immediately seen to be distorted upward as we would expect. This fact is independent of K and therefore of the particular equilibrium configuration under consideration.

The equilibrium condition $y = h(c,K)$ allows us to conclude that with y held fixed,

$$\frac{dc}{dK} = -h_K/h_c.$$

It is then simply a matter of computation to show that

$$\frac{dc}{dK} = \frac{1}{4} \cdot \frac{(1 - 2y + 2c)}{(1 - y + c)} > 0,$$

and that with y held fixed,

$$\frac{du}{dK} = -\frac{1}{4} \cdot \frac{(1 - 2y + 2c)}{(y - c)} < 0.$$

If the equilibrium is shifted by increasing K, then distortion in terms of excessive consumption of highly observable goods increases for everyone, regardless of his other income. Moreover, everyone is made worse off by increases in K and the shift in the

---

2. The substitution which makes the equation directly integrable is

$$r(c) = 1 - 2h(c) - 2c.$$

Having made the substitution, the result follows directly by integrating and then substituting back for h.

equilibrium which goes with that increase. This again holds regardless of income. The magnitude of the losses may vary over income levels. Increases in K produce Pareto inferior equilibrium configurations of the market. This is a conclusion reached in the context of the labor market. Presumably, everyone would vote to reduce K if that were possible. Moreover, one can now see more clearly why the signaling game is similar to the coordination game with multiple nonequivalent equilibria. For each K, there is a stable equilibrium in the market. There are many of them. Reductions in K lead to equilibria in which signaling still takes place, but in which everyone is better off. This corresponds to moving up the diagonal in the diagram presented earlier.

The status signaling model works, that is to say, signaling takes place, because the real opportunity costs of signaling via conspicuous consumption are negatively correlated with income, which is what consumption is supposed to signal. This is the analogue of the condition that education costs must be negatively correlated with productive capabilities in the labor market in order for effective signaling to take place.

9 Loans and Household Credit

The market for household loans has an information structure similar in many ways to that of the job market. The bank or lending institution buys an uncertain future stream of payments with cash now. The household buys cash now with its ability and willingness to pay back on a regular basis in the future. The bank, like the employer, buys a lottery. It cannot directly observe the individual's ability to pay back, but it does have a plethora of potentially useful personal data on the individual or household. The decision is whether or not to grant the loan request and what interest rate to charge, the analogues of the hiring and the wage decisions in the job market.

Individual attributes formally divide into those which are alterable and those which are not, that is to say, into potential signals and potential indices. Potential signals may be altered by the loan applicant in order to project a favorable credit image. The informational content of potential signals and indices is determined by the market equilibrium, which in turn depends upon the conditional probabilistic beliefs of the loan-granting institution.

At this point, it is useful to digress briefly to describe how the modern loan-granting institution processes personal data, returning to the general features of the market's informational structure later.

The observable data used by credit-granting institutions tend to be along the lines suggested in the following list.[1]

Personal Data Used in Evaluating Credit Risk

1. age
2. telephone
3. income
4. living status (who lives in the household)
5. bank accounts
6. time at present address and past address
7. marital status
8. occupation
9. department store references
10. zip code
11. size of loan request
12. bank branch
13. home ownership and other assets
14. liquidity of assets.

The credit institution uses these data in the following way. It gives the individual applicant a score on each attribute, and then it takes a weighted average of these scores to get an overall score. The score is used to make the loan decision. If the score is sufficiently high, the loan is granted. This may not sound as if the bank bases its decisions upon a conditional probability over the loan's profitability, given the observable data. But, in fact, the scoring system is very close to the use of full conditional probabilities. Since this is methodologically important, let us investigate it further.

Derivation of the Scoring Scheme

Let r be a random variable representing return on a loan. Let X be a vector of scores on various observable attributes. A statistician, using historical loan records for the bank, develops estimates for the mean and variance-covariance matrix for the

1. See Thomas E. Caywood, "Point Scoring for Credit Customers," *Banking*, October 1970.

vector (r,X). The mean is $(\bar{r},\bar{X})$ and the variance-covariance matrix is

$$\begin{pmatrix} a & b^T \\ b & C \end{pmatrix}. \tag{9.1}$$

Now the statistical scoring problem is simply that of finding a new random variable s, a weighted sum of the $(X - \bar{X})$'s, which is as highly correlated with $(r - \bar{r})$ as possible:

$$s = \alpha^T(X - \bar{X}). \tag{9.2}$$

The weights α are chosen so as to make the variances of s and r the same. Subject to this constraint, they want to maximize $cov((r - \bar{r}),s)$.

More formally, the problem is to

$$\max_{\alpha} \alpha^T b \quad \text{subject to} \quad \alpha^T C\alpha = a. \tag{9.3}$$

The solution is easily computed to be

$$\bar{\alpha} = \left(\frac{a}{b^T C^{-1}b}\right)^{1/2} C^{-1}b. \tag{9.4}$$

Any other linear combination of the X's which is uncorrelated with s is also uncorrelated with r, and hence totally uninformative.

There remains the question of how much one loses by employing only the summary statistic s in assessing the conditional probability of r. The following proposition goes some way toward answering that question.

Proposition: If (r,X) is jointly normal and s is defined as above, then the conditional distribution of r given X is normal and is identical to the conditional distribution of r given s.

Proof: We suppose (r,X) has mean $(\bar{r},\bar{X})$ and variance-covariance matrix $\begin{pmatrix} a & b^T \\ b & C \end{pmatrix}$. It is well known that the conditional distribution of r given X is normal with mean[2]

2. M. Pratt, H. Raiffa, R. Schlaiffer, *Introduction to Statistical Decision Theory* (New York: McGraw-Hill, 1965) gives the derivation.

$$\bar{r} + b^T C^{-1}(X - \overline{X}), \qquad (9.5)$$

and variance

$$a - b^T C^{-1} b. \qquad (9.6)$$

The joint distribution of r and s is normal with mean $(\bar{r}, \Sigma a_i \overline{X}_i)$ and variance-covariance matrix $\begin{pmatrix} a & \alpha^T b \\ \alpha^T b & \alpha^T C \alpha \end{pmatrix}$. Hence, the conditional distribution of r given s is normal with mean

$$\bar{r} + \frac{\alpha^T b}{\alpha^T C \alpha}(s - \bar{s}), \qquad (9.7)$$

and variance

$$a - \frac{(\alpha^T b)^2}{\alpha^T C \alpha}. \qquad (9.8)$$

But substituting for α in (9.7) and (9.8) yields (9.5) and (9.6) respectively. This completes the proof.

Thus, in the case of the normal distribution, using the score to generate a conditional distribution for r costs nothing in terms of lost information. The score has the obvious advantage that it is conceptually easier to use for loan assessors.

Credit Institutions

The scoring scheme just described is not a theoretical construction. Versions of it are actually used by modern credit institutions. The people who decide on the loan do not actually think in terms of a probability distribution over r given s. Rather, they are given a cutoff level s^*, which can be varied with economic conditions.[3] The statisticians continually update

3. It is clear, I think, that if the decision is simply to grant or not to grant the loan, the form of the optimal decision will be:

Grant, if $s \gtrless s^*$,

Do not grant, if $s < s^*$,

for some level of s^*.

estimates of means, variances, and covariances as new market data come in. The point is simply that modern credit institutions effectively use conditional probabilistic assessments derived from past market data to decide whether to grant credit, and on what terms. The method is usually some variant of the scoring scheme described above. Thus at least some receivers of signals interpret them in the manner assumed in the model of market signaling.

The Informational Structure of the Market

It is not difficult to see that most, if not all, of the items on the list of personal data used by credit institutions are alterable, and hence potential signals. This might suggest that the informational structure of the market is like that of the *educational* signaling case. And to some extent it is. A person can certainly manipulate his portfolio to increase the liquidity of his assets, if that will be favorably interpreted. Moreover, the costs of generating liquid assets are probably highly correlated with wealth or income and hence ability to repay. One would expect this sort of active signaling from wealthy individuals or corporations who, not surprisingly, can borrow at more favorable rates than the rest of us.

At a more modest level, individuals can acquire a telephone, establish previous credit at department stores and the like, and invest in a favorable credit rating by being reliable and punctual in repaying debts. Again the costs of so conducting oneself, both psychic and real, are likely to be negatively correlated with the likelihood that one will default.

The sophisticated individual might even invest in his future ability to borrow by borrowing now, putting the money in a savings account, and repaying the entire loan on schedule. If the loan rate is 12% and the savings account returns 5%, the cost of a thousand dollar loan for a year would be $70.00 — not a bad investment, if it makes borrowing on favorable terms easier indefinitely into the future.

There are, then, elements of active signaling behavior in the market. Yet it is clear, on reflection, that many potentially alterable characteristics such as home ownership and marital status are not in fact the subject of active signaling in the loan market. Such characteristics, then, function in the market as though they were indices. Since indices have already been observed to function in several different ways in the job markets, it is not necessary to review them exhaustively here. One might look for situations in which indices pass statistical information, or for situations in which they cause different groups to settle into different signaling equilibria.

The reason that many potential signals turn into effective indices is that the costs of altering them swamp the gains. Thus, even when banks and other credit institutions react to them, it is not worth investing in them. It is difficult, for example, to imagine someone marrying purely for the purpose of appearing to a bank to be a stable family type.

One's previous borrowing record is a potentially important signal. This means that people who have trouble getting credit at the start will never acquire the requisite signal in terms of a favorable borrowing record. Alternatively, if the young person's wealth is low, he may have to go to loan sharks, pay high interest rates, and hence run a greater risk of default. If he defaults, that goes on his record and he has trouble borrowing in the future. There may be a kind of vicious cycle associated with variations in the initial wealth of individuals or their families. Lack of assets or backing leads to an inability to borrow to acquire assets, which leads in turn to a continued inability to borrow on all but the least favorable terms.

Notice that it is not necessary to argue that assets are signals by themselves, although they probably are. Assets are guarantees, that is to say, ways of reducing the loss in case of default. The wealthier young person has an easier time establishing a good credit rating because he has the guarantee which enables him to get credit initially. Assets are also an index — that is to say, negatively correlated with defaults — because the person with assets does not have to default and hence, because the future cost of a default now is high, will tend not to default. Assets then are both a guarantee and an index.

In credit markets we find an informational structure analogous to that of the job market. At first glance, there appears to be less opportunity for active signaling in the loan markets.[4] Those things which are potential signals tend to take on the character of indices, because the costs of alteration exceed the gains. If there are discriminatory phenomena implicit in the loan market informational structure, they will tend to be either of the statistical kind or associated with variable signaling costs.

To summarize the discussion, assessing and establishing credit is a signaling game. Credit institutions rely on attributes which are informative and develop scoring schemes which are surrogates for conditional distributions over individual reliability, given the observable attributes. The normal distinction between signals and indices holds. But many potential signals such as house ownership and income are sufficiently costly to manipulate relative to the gains that they act like indices. Nevertheless there are real signals. Owning a telephone is one. Bank branch, address, liquidity of assets, and kinds of bank accounts are others.[5]

4. Both the relative importance of various signals and indices, as measured by their weights in the scoring function, and the extent to which there is active signaling in the market are subjects worthy of detailed empirical investigation.

5. The use of scoring in the evaluation of credit risk by banks and other credit institutions is discussed in three articles: Thomas E. Caywood, "Point Scoring for Credit Customers," *Banking,* October 1970; Nicolas Johnson, "How Point Scoring Can Do More Than Help Make Loan Decisions," *Banking,* August 1971; William Bogess, "Screen Test Your Credit Risks," *Harvard Business Review,* November 1967. The statistics of finding the weights to generate the score are discussed in T. W. Anderson, *An Introduction to Multivariate Statistical Analysis* (New York: John Wiley, 1958). The assertions concerning conditional distributions for jointly normal variables are proved in Pratt, Raiffa, and Schlaiffer, *Introduction to Statistical Decision Theory.*

10 Selective Admissions, Screening, and Promotion

There is a range of quasi-market selective screening phenomena, ranging from college admissions to promotion in large organizations, that have the informational structure of the job market and hence can usefully be viewed through the same conceptual lens. The purpose of this chapter is not to dispose of these subjects. It is rather to suggest ways in which the phenomena can usefully be viewed as signaling games with equilibria, defined in terms of a feedback loop.

Promotion in Large Organizations

A principal problem in modern management and organization theory is what is known as the incentive problem. Individual managers have goals which do not necessarily correspond with those of the organization. The prescriptive management problem is that of designing reward schemes so that managers pursuing their own ends will make efficient decisions from the point of view of the organization.

There are several different aspects of the problem, corresponding to different aspects of efficient organizational performance. One is the coordination problem among departments or subsections of the organization. Organizations are almost by definition decentralized decision-making entities. The problem then becomes that of so rewarding performance that the desired degree of coordinated decision-making is achieved. Coordination, of course, requires communication. Hence, inducing flows of accurate and useful information is a primary concern of the manager.

Joseph Bower, in a recent work on resource allocation within the firm, describes this aspect of the problem well. He is speaking in the context of investment planning in an organization.

It is well documented that the way in which performance is rewarded influences the process of providing forecasts against which performance is measured. In other words, when planning data are used to measure managers, they influence the character of the plans. It is one thing to take account of this fact theoretically by providing for the phenomena in the concept of structural context. It is another problem to use performance measurement to reward successful managers without distorting the communication of information up and down the hierarchy, for purposes of planning.[1]

Bower is arguing that plans themselves, and not just performance, must be evaluated if resource allocation distortion is to be minimized.

One could go on to review a rather large literature on the incentive and informational problems of organizations. But I prefer to stop and state my own view as to where the critical trade-off occurs in evaluating and rewarding managerial performance.

The typical manager, I would argue, focuses upon promotion as his primary goal. Promotion means increased power, prestige, and usually income. Given the methods by which managers are evaluated for promotion, the manager will invest in those activities which are taken as signals of ability to handle higher-level jobs. Doing an about-face, one can consider the same situation from the organizational point of view. The problem is that there are two problems. One is achieving the maximum possible efficiency in the allocation of nonhuman re-

1. Joseph Bower, *Managing the Resource Allocation Process* (Boston: Graduate School of Business Administration, Harvard University, 1970).

sources in any prescribed time period. The other is the allocation of human resources: the promotion of good people.[2]

We have in fact an internal signaling game, or, rather, hundreds of them. Junior people invest in activities which win them high marks in terms of promotion. Senior management interprets signals, evaluates people, and promotes some of them. Effective signals are those which have the properties described in the job market, ones which significantly affect probabilistic assessments of managerial ability.

Maximizing short-run profits may be a very good signal of management capability in a manager, because good managers find it easier to achieve high short-run profits than do less-talented managers. If short-run profits are taken as a signal (and they may be a good one), then people will invest in them, which in turn may badly distort the investment decisions in the organization. Effective signals of managerial talent, if used by top management, may distort the nonhuman resource allocation in the organization. Conversely, if certain potentially useful signals are ignored in order to avoid this distortion, the screening for top management will be less effective, and human resource allocation will suffer.

There is a direct trade-off here. The senior executive is continually operating in a second-best world. To deal adequately with the problem, he must understand the strategic elements in the ongoing signaling game. His strategic decisions concern which signals to respond to. Unlike the employer in the job market, he may choose not to react to certain kinds of potential signals, because to do so would be to distort the resource alloca-

2. The reader who is familiar with a remarkable little book, *The Peter Principle*, by Hull and Peter, will recognize a relation between their work and this chapter. The underlying premise of the model of rising to one's level of incompetence is that those responsible for promotion ignore the human resource allocation process and the signaling game which accompanies it. Indeed, people are promoted on the basis of demonstrated competence in lower-level jobs. They simply do not look for signals of ability to do higher-level jobs. Put this way, it seems an extreme assumption. Nevertheless, their empirical findings suggest that there are real trade-offs between efficiency in the human and nonhuman resource allocation processes.

tion process. The employer in the job market does not care whether people overinvest in education. But the senior executive does care if his managers overinvest in short-run division profits or in writing literate briefs. He can and should exercise self-conscious control over the way the signaling game is played.

The extent to which the demands for effective signals and for nondistortionary evaluative criteria are in conflict is an empirical matter. But because of the somewhat peculiar attributes that make an activity an effective signal, there is no good reason to expect, a priori, that no conflict will occur. If only activities which further the ends of the organization are rewarded by promotion, lower-level managers will invest in these activities. This will solve the resource allocation problem (Bower's work makes it clear that it is not that simple), but it may lead to the promotion of the wrong people. Or, what is more likely, it may fail effectively to distinguish people at all, so that the promotion process contains a large element of randomness in it.

It will help the manager to know that the signaling game over which he presides may have multiple equilibria. The extent of overinvestment in short-run profits by division heads will vary with the equilibrium. It may be possible for the senior executive to act unilaterally to shift the equilibrium so as to reduce the level of overinvestment while retaining divisional profits as a signal, if that proves useful.

Selective Admissions Procedures

The logical structure of the signaling game involved in admissions contexts is essentially no different from the job market. Relatively large groups of applicants are selected for positions in colleges and graduate schools on the basis of a variety of signals and indices ranging from interviews to test scores and previous educational performance. There is no need, at this stage, to review the elements in the signaling game. Let me confine myself to some remarks about selective admissions problems, which stem from viewing the procedure through the conceptual lens of the job market model.

1. The distinction between signals and indices is important. Education is a signal in many admissions contexts. Students can invest in it. Test scores, on the other hand, are probably most appropriately viewed as indices, although a certain amount of "preparation" is possible.

2. The overinvestment problem arises with respect to education. At several levels one frequently hears complaints, from those concerned with undergraduate education, that the post-graduate admissions game distorts the investment of student time and energy at the undergraduate level. Students avoid courses in unfamiliar subjects, or they study too hard or in the wrong areas. The signaling game is seen as working against the aims of a liberal arts education.

Without arguing the pros and cons of this type of education, there seems little doubt that the exigencies of graduate admissions, including professional schools, make student effort a process of investing in privately productive signals. And it is not at all clear that, abstracted from the signaling game, the effort is worth it — that is to say, that the education acquired for signaling purposes contributes much to either private or social productivity or welfare.

These equilibria shift over time. Currently, medical school is an increasingly popular option. Hence the equilibrium levels of investment in premed courses and grades have shifted upward in recent years.

Another area in which the signaling game may have detrimental side effects is at the high school level. From reasonably early ages, students are guided through courses of study designed to make them look like good bets (lotteries) to colleges. The expenditure of student effort, and the concomitant anxiety over a prolonged period, may constitute a large diversion of human resources and energies away from relatively productive activities at early ages.

3. It was suggested that tests are best thought of as indices. If we are concerned about overinvestment in education or in grades, it is natural to think in terms of relying more heavily upon indices which cannot be invested in or overinvested in (or

at least not to the same extent). Tests have this property. They may also be powerful sources of additional information.

But there are dangers. Some are more real than others. The reader may wish to think in terms of suppressing signals like education in favor of indices like tests.

One problem is that education is a source of information, a real signal. Hence there is a trade-off between quality of information (and the resultant quality and fairness of resource allocation) and the reduction of unproductive investment in signals.

Second, some people (a) do badly on tests (at least tests as we currently know them), and (b) know this from experience. Such people might argue that a system which relies solely on tests is discriminatory. They would have a better chance in a multidimensional signaling system. Now there is a sense in which all imperfect screening devices discriminate against those who are excluded in this world and would not have been in a world of perfect information. Nevertheless, to argue for the multisignal system is essentially to argue for reducing the probability of error in the imperfect system. Hence the problem really reduces to the first one: to throw away a signal is to throw away information. Nevertheless, to do so may still be beneficial.

Third, tests are asserted to be culturally biased. Cultural bias really emerges in the way tests are used, and not in tests themselves.

A test score is a random variable. For each level of underlying characteristics, the score has a conditional distribution. Turning it around, a conditional distribution of capability is given to each score. The power of the test as a signal depends upon how much the conditional distribution shifts when the score changes. The cultural bias problem arises because there may be very good reasons why the distribution of talent conditional on scores will differ systematically over two groups.

At this point some notation will be useful. Let $n =$ a measure of some kind of capability, $s =$ test score, and $p(n|s)$ be a conditional distribution of $n|s$. Now the assertion is that there may be two groups A and B, such that

$$p_A(n|s) \neq p_B(n|s).$$

If q_A and q_B are the proportions of A and B in the population, then the overall conditional distribution of $n|s$ is

$$p(n|s) = q_A p_A(n|s) + q_B p_B(n|s).$$

The test may be used in a culturally biased way if all people are evaluated using $p(n|s)$, when some underlying causal factor makes

$$p_A(n|s) \neq p_B(n|s).$$

Notice that $p_A(n|s)$ can diverge from $p_B(n|s)$ in many different ways. For example, they may differ only in terms of their means. Alternatively, the means may be the same, but $p_A(n|s)$ is much "tighter" than $p_B(n|s)$. In the second case, s is just a more powerful signal for group A than for group B.

The solution to the problem of "culturally biased" tests is not necessarily to eliminate them, although that is certainly one strategy. The problem really is to identify the source of the bias and interpret the scores correctly. The problem of cultural bias arises when an institution fails to pay attention to an index in cases when, for the sake of fairness, it ought to.

Optional Signaling Systems

Discretionary use of signals and indices has some obvious attractions. It allows the individual to select criteria on which he or she feels at a comparative advantage and to eliminate others on which he or she feels at a comparative disadvantage. It may also, as in the case of optional pass-fail grades, free people to undertake activities into which they would not otherwise venture. In other words, it may partially solve the overinvestment problem. All of this, of course, is bought at some informational cost.

Several factors determine the extent of the diminution in the flow of relevant information. One is the extent to which individuals can predict their performance beforehand. A second concerns when the individual has to choose. For example, if students opt for pass-fail before the course begins, the informational loss is less than that which occurs if the decision is based upon the students' observation of a letter grade. One occasionally hears that making grades optional will eliminate grades as an informational source. But this is simply not true. In fact the problem may be that pass-fail and similar optional procedures *are not a strong enough disincentive* to distortionary overinvestment in a narrow range of courses. This is particularly true of the highly competitive quasi-market for places in graduate and professional schools.

There are other potential effects of optional signals. On the average, discretionary control over the signals emitted is likely to lower the signaling costs to the individual by allowing him to avoid very high-cost activities. The equilibrium effect of a general reduction in marginal costs of signals may well be an escalation in the levels of investment and therefore bring little or no reduction in the overall costs.

The problem of designing socially acceptable selection procedures is far too large to be dealt with adequately here. However, it is to be emphasized that the signaling model suggests rather strongly that the problem is not simply that of finding ways to obtain the best possible information.

The Composition of the Group Problem

It is sometimes argued that admissions problems are complicated by the fact that the composition of the group matters. The analogue in the case of the firm is the fact that the individual's marginal product depends upon the levels of all the firm's inputs: capital, labor, and so on. The reader is perhaps concerned that this kind of interdependence will alter the signaling game in some fundamental way, but it does not. Admissions committees do care about the distribution of abilities, talents, personalities, and cultural backgrounds in the groups they admit, and this affects the applicants' worth to the institutions and hence the rewards to various types of signaling activity. But basically, signals are informative about individual characteristics and the game retains its logical structure.

It is true, however, that if there are several institutions, or several geographical regions, individuals will select the institution and the region as well as a signaling strategy. To analyze this fully, a multiple-market model is required. In an appendix, an attempt is made to show that the multiple-market case lends itself to the same kind of analysis. In any given market, the compositions of both the applicant and the admitted groups are determined endogenously in the model. The notion that individuals and groups self-select themselves out of markets is of great potential importance and is discussed further under the heading of discrimination.

Competition for a Fixed Number of Places

There is one feature of a selective admissions process which, when found, does affect the signaling game. It is the fact that there may be a fixed number of places for which individuals are competing. The effect on the signaling game is to eliminate the multiple equilibria. Since the effect is of some intellectual interest, I shall illustrate it with an example, though I do not find it of overwhelming importance. Let me explain why. What is at issue is not whether there are a fixed number of places in a given institution (for example, the Harvard Law School), but whether there are a fixed number of places for which a particular type of signaling activity is a useful investment. Hence, undergraduate grades are a signal to Harvard Law, but also to other law schools, graduate schools, and most other employers in the society.

The Example

Suppose that the payoff to being admitted to some institution is V, and the payoff to rejection is U. There is an unobservable characteristic n, representing ability, and an observable and alterable attribute y with alteration costs y/n, which depend on n. The distribution of n in the population of potential applicants is $r(n)$. The admitting institution believes that n is a nondecreasing functions of y, and sets a cutoff level $\bar{y}$ for admission. If $y \geqq \bar{y}$, the person is admitted, otherwise not.

The individual with ability n will set $y = \bar{y}$ and be admitted if

$$V - \frac{\bar{y}}{n} \geqq U.$$

Otherwise, he will set $y = 0$ and stay out. Thus, the people who stay in are those with ability level n such that

$$n \geqq \frac{\bar{y}}{V - U}.$$

But there may not be sufficient places for them. In equilibrium, there will be. The condition is:

$$\int_{\frac{\bar{y}}{V-U}}^{\infty} r(n)\, dn = \text{the number of available places.}$$

The condition simply says that in equilibrium, applicants must not be misinformed about the cutoff level. The additional condition determines $\bar{y}$. In equilibrium, the admitting institution will find that the conditional distribution of n in the group admitted is

$$\frac{r(n)}{\displaystyle\int_{\frac{\bar{y}}{V-U}}^{\infty} r(n)\, dn},$$

for $n \geqq \dfrac{\bar{y}}{v - u}$. But since the institution is merely concerned with filling $\bar{x}$ slots with the best people it can find, this distribution plays no essential role.

The signaling equilibrium in this model is therefore unique, in sharp contrast to the job market model and the status model. However, as soon as we drop the absolute constraint on numbers and introduce more institutions with available positions, even if they are of lesser prestige, or alternative spots for which y may be an effective signal, then the determinateness of the equilibrium disappears. In that case there will be many $\bar{y}$'s corresponding to the many institutions. Given the $\bar{y}$'s for all but one institution, the $\bar{y}$ of the remaining one is determined. But together they will be indeterminate.

To illustrate, suppose that the parameter U in the model depended upon n. In fact, suppose that lying behind U is a signaling game in which y is also a signal. If that game is open-ended, as the job markets were, then U will depend upon n *and* an indeterminate parameter K. Denote this by $U(n,K)$. The equilibrium $\bar{y}$ in the example depends upon U and thus derivatively upon K. With a particular K, one has a particular $\bar{y}$. Thus the multiple equilibria return in the form of a locus of admissible pairs $(\bar{y},K)$. It is only when one institution is isolated that the absolute numbers constraint determines the equilibrium uniquely.

If the educational signaling model of Chapter 3 is reinterpreted to cover admissions, and if the number of positions correspond to the number of people in Group II in that model, then all the equilibria in the model would be equilibria in the admissions signaling game. Hence competition for limited positions does not necessarily eliminate the multiplicity of equilibria.

The general principle covering the relationship between limited positions and multiple signaling equilibria is simply that the two are compatible when and where there are multiple signaling equilibria all of which lead to the same allocation of people to positions. There are at least two distinct situations which cause this phenomenon. One, as exemplified by the early job market models, is a situation in which the allocation of people to positions is literally insensitive to shifts in the signaling equilibrium. The other is a situation in which shifts in one screening procedure cause shifts in another. This can occur even when there are limited positions available in each sphere. The equilibrium in the system taken as a whole will be arbitrary.

Equilibrium is determined uniquely in situations in which (a) the procedure is isolated so that shifts in the environment do not cause shifts in the pattern of applications, and (b) the number of applicants is sensitive to shifts in the admission standards. An example might be competition for promotion inside a large organization, the organization itself being a relatively isolated unit.

11 Guarantees

Guarantees are pervasive phenomena. Sometimes they have a signaling function in the market. Guarantees are most common in markets for large or expensive consumer durables, where there is a well-defined event called a breakdown. A breakdown eliminates completely the flow of services from the good to the consumer. A breakdown can be thought of as a random move by nature against the consumer. One purpose of a guarantee is to alter the payoff to the consumer in case of a breakdown. The alteration increases the expected utility of owning the good and presumably raises the price which the seller can charge. If one thinks of the good as a lottery and a guarantee as a change in one of the payoffs, then a good with a guarantee and one without are just different goods.

Thus far there is no signaling. Why then might a guarantee be an effective signal of product reliability? To answer this, let us return briefly to educational signaling in the job market. A rather crude but accurate description of the pure educational signaling model would be that people go out and buy something useless but observable in order to signal their competence. It works because the cost of the thing they buy is negatively correlated with their productive potential. When education is productive, the prescription still holds. Buy more of it than is productive if it is less costly to you. Again, the amount purchased is an effective signal if costs are negatively correlated with capability.

Guarantees can be seen in this light. The expected cost of a guarantee to the seller (and signaler) is negatively correlated with the probability of a breakdown on any given machine randomly selected. Thus if any spectrum can be found along which to make the guarantee more comprehensive or of longer duration, guarantee levels along the spectrum should act as signals. And indeed they do. When General Motors went from 5 year/ 50 thousand mile guarantees in 1968 to 2 year/24 thousand miles in 1969, the cries of "planned obsolescence" and "motorized junk" were ubiquitous. The message could hardly have been clearer. The guarantee, then, may have a secondary signaling effect along with its primary effect upon payoffs.

The signaling effect is upon the consumer's assessment of a probability of a breakdown. The more comprehensive the guarantee, the lower the probability and the higher the expected utility from purchasing the good.

The consumer is in the refrigerator market less frequently than the employer is in the job market. Hence the informational feedback which closes the loop in the job market is less complete here. But the consumer may generalize across products, especially if they are products from the same firm. When he infers probabilities of breakdowns from guarantees using other market experience, we have the signaling externalities of the job market, at least to some extent. If these are present, and firms are treated as averages, then there may be multiple signaling equilibria in guarantees.

One must not carry the analogy too far. For one thing, quality control (and hence the probability of a breakdown) is a decision variable for the producer. Competition can and does occur on the durability spectrum. Second, the consumer may intellectualize the message of the guarantee by reasoning from the guarantee to the expected cost to the guarantor. In other words, even when market experience is limited, the consumer may reason that the cost of the guarantee varies with the reliability of the product and draw the appropriate and desired conclusion. This will produce a certain amount of randomness in the interpretation of the message. In the job market, the employer's beliefs were firmly tied down by market experience.

Another feature of guarantee signaling is the problem of defining precisely when the guarantee is applicable. A breakdown is a relatively clearcut event. Beyond that one might try to guarantee levels of performance for a product. In general there is a problem of operationally defining such levels so as to make it possible to determine when they have been met (or not met). This tends to leave length of guarantee period as the most usual continuous dimension. In special cases, there are others. Tire tread allows prorated guarantees on tires. In general, a clearcut event such as a breakdown is needed. If an art gallery guaranteed customer satisfaction on its sales, one could run an art museum in one's home for nothing. The need for an operational test to determine when a guarantee applies limits the scope of its use.

A guarantee is insurance. The premium is buried in the price. The seller sells the good and an insurance policy. The argument of the last few paragraphs, then, is that it matters from whom you buy the insurance. The insurer may or may not have inside information. When he is the seller, there is a presumption that he does. Hence one's assessment of the likelihood of the event is affected by the insurance policy offered. The situation is like buying life insurance from the airline before the flight or the surgeon before the operation.

Finally, guarantees as signals are to be sharply distinguished from conventional signaling codes.[1] An example might prove helpful. An employment agency may (in fact many do) send people to jobs along with assessments of their capabilities. Now they might try to guarantee them in order to improve business. That would be one strategy. But even without a guarantee, their reports might be believable only because they have been relatively accurate and informative in the past. The latter is a conventionally based signaling code. There are no immediate costs to lying. But since both buyer and seller are in the market

1. Conventional signaling is defined and discussed extensively by David K. Lewis [1969].

often and over a long time, the employer can learn the code and the seller invest in his signaling reputation.

Another example of a conventional signaling code is ski-reporting. Ski resorts phone in reports on snow conditions which are broadcast as a public service throughout the season. Although the reports are somewhat vague, they do bear some relationship to the truth and hence they are informative. Skiers are in the market often enough to learn the signaling code, and resorts invest in acquiring a signaling reputation because of the long-run benefits from being able to communicate. Unlike most of the signaling phenomena we have discussed, the power of the signal does not derive from the immediate and direct cost that sending it imposes on the signaler.

12 Used Cars and the Absence of Effective Signaling

Sometimes one finds a market in which there is a clearcut informational asymmetry and considerable buyer uncertainty, but no effective signaling takes place. Since the absence of information flows affects the performance of the market as much as the presence of effective signaling, it is useful to inquire into the circumstances that make signaling of the type observed in job markets unlikely or impossible.

A useful example is the private market for used cars. By private market I mean the nondealer market. The effect of buyer uncertainty here has been analyzed by George Akerlof.[1] Akerlof's model begins from the plausible premise that sellers of used cars know more about the product than buyers, at least prior to any transaction. For ease of exposition, assume that demand is a function of price p and average quality of cars in the market, μ. We denote demand by $D(\mu,p)$. It is assumed that consumers have a reasonably good idea about μ when they enter the market, but with respect to a particular car, they are not certain. The signs of the derivatives are,

$$D_1 > 0, \quad D_2 < 0.$$

1. G. A. Akerlof, "The Market for 'Lemons': Qualitative Uncertainty and the Market Mechanism," *Quarterly Journal of Economics,* Vol. 84, August 1970.

It is assumed that supply and average quality are upward slop-ing functions of price. As price falls, nonlemon owners with-draw their cars, leaving the lemons on the market.

Equilibrium in the market is determined by

$$D(\mu(p),p) = S(p).$$

One possible situation is depicted in Figure 12.1. Because of the presence of $\mu(p)$ as an argument in the demand function, the demand schedule may rise and then fall as a function of p.

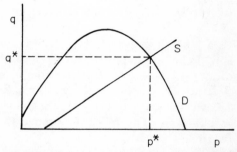

Figure 12.1. Market Equilibrium with Buyer Uncertainty

It is now not difficult to see that multiple equilibria are pos-sible as in Figure 12.2a, or the complete collapse of the market as in Figure 12.2b.

Now the nonlemon owners have an obvious incentive to communicate, just as the high-productivity types do in the job market. In fact, they are in relatively similar positions. Barring dealers, used car sellers are in the market relatively infrequently. They are treated by buyers as averages, just as job applicants are. The problem in the car market is that there is nothing with which to signal. Recall what this means. It means there is noth-ing the used car buyer can purchase at reasonable cost that is visible and whose costs are correlated with the quality of his car. Verbal declarations are costless and therefore useless. Any-one can lie about why he is selling the car. One can offer to let the buyer have the car checked. The lemon owner can make the

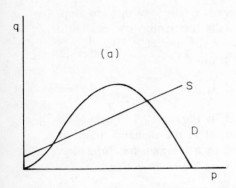 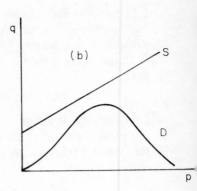

Figure 12.2. Alternative Market Equilibria

same offer. It's a bluff. If called, nothing is lost. Besides, such checks are costly. Reliability reports from the owner's mechanic are untrustworthy. The clever nonlemon owner might pay for the checkup but let the purchaser choose the inspector. The problem for the owner, then, is to keep the inspection cost down. Guarantees do not work. The seller may move to Cleveland, leaving no forwarding address.

In short, there is not much the nonlemon owner can do that the lemon owner cannot imitate. Signaling by and large breaks down, and the Akerlof effects are observed. It is notable that, for some models, used car dealer prices run as much as 50% higher than the private market's prices as quoted in the want ads.[2] Dealers, of course, can (1) give guarantees which probably have a high signal value and (2) have a reputation to establish and protect.[3]

The informational incentive structure of the used car market is much like the job market. But there appears to be a paucity

2. This observation comes from reading want ads in several newspapers in several cities and comparing prices there with dealer prices. The proposition applies most to relatively high-quality foreign cars.

3. The dealer functions at least in part as an informational intermediary. His enhanced signaling capability over the private seller stems from this persistent presence in the market and the consequent ability to build and maintain a reputation for quality control. In addition to guarantees, dealer signaling will take place through the setting of prices.

of effective signals. An effective signal would be an activity (a) which costs more, the lower the quality of the car, and (b) whose costs do not simply swamp the gains from signaling quality to the consumer. This suggests a role for an informational intermediary, an institution which inspects cars and sells certified quality ratings. To stay in business, such an organization would establish a reputation for accurate ratings. Ratings need not be a simple score, but rather a set of scores on different attributes. Lemon owners would not get a rating, but that would not destroy the new informational source in the market. There would just be a residue of relatively low-quality, unrated cars in the market equilibrium.

One can imagine the seller selecting the manner in which his car is tested and rated. It could be just excellent, good, fair, or poor. For more money, he could get more detailed information. He can have maintenance work done at a garage before the rating test. The cost will, of course, depend upon the initial state of the car. Carrying it one step further, it is possible that the seller could go to the rating agency, ask them to bring the quality of the car up to a certain standard, and then certify it.

The informational function of the rating organization would be like that of the educational institution in the job market. It sells something whose unit cost decreases with the quality of the product. It may even change the quality of the product in the course of its activity.

There may be jobs and job markets for which there are no effective signals either. Education costs, for example, will not be correlated with all types of productive capability. In such cases, if indices also fail, the Akerlof model applies. It predicts that there may be multiple equilibria or that the bottom may fall out of the market.

The Akerlof model transferred to job markets is reminiscent of a more elaborate model of wage determination and discrimination proposed by Kenneth Arrow.[4]

4. K. J. Arrow, "Models of Discrimination," in A. H. Pascal, ed., *Racial Discrimination in Economic Life* (Lexington, Mass.: D. C. Heath, 1972). I shall discuss a simplified version of it, for expositional purposes. The interested reader should consult the original for a full account.

Professor Arrow noted that an individual's efforts on the job, and hence his success at performing it, may be correlated with the wage. This implies that average quality depends on the wage. And the equilibrium wage depends upon the average quality of work done. The situation is pictured in Figure 12.3. Its kinship to the Akerlof model is clear.

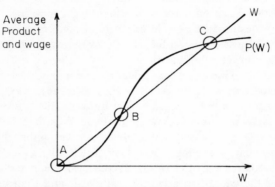

Figure 12.3. Multiple Equilibria in the Wage Feedback Model

As drawn, there are three equilibria. Points A and C are stable. At A, there are no transactions on the market. Point B is an unstable equilibrium. Now the interesting thing is that if there are two identifiable groups and this mechanism applies separately to each, they may end up in different equilibria. The argument is essentially that given in Chapter 4 in discussing the interaction of educational signaling and race. Averages are taken by employers over people who look the same. The observability of the characteristic defining the groups is sufficient to set limits to the external effects of the performance of any given individual. Hence it is possible to find discrimination based on differences in the equilibrium configuration of two identifiable groups. In fact, if one group ends up at A, the phenomenon looks like occupational exclusion.

To summarize the discussion, the following points are relevant.

1. An understanding of the structure of the signaling game in the job market may help explain the absence of effective signaling in other markets. The used car market is an example.

2. The effect of asymmetrical uncertainty between buyers and sellers as to product quality may make quality as well as quantity supplied a function of price. This, in conjunction with the absence of effective signals, may lead to discrete multiple equilibria or the nonexistence of the market.

3. A simplified version of the Arrow wage feedback model has a similar structure. Signals are absent. But indices may still play a role if there are multiple equilibria. Different groups may end up in different equilibria. The source of impact of indices is much as it was in the job market signaling game. Here the response is automatic and not the result of signaling decisions by individuals.

13 Discriminatory Mechanisms in Market Signaling

Considerable attention has already been devoted in passing to discriminatory aspects of the market signaling games under consideration. Indeed, it is not possible to acknowledge the informational role of observable unalterable characteristics without bumping into potential sources of discrimination in the information system.

The educational signaling model produced multiple equilibria. When observable and unalterable characteristics are appended to that model, multiple equilibria turn into potential arbitrary differences in the signaling equilibrium configuration of two or more observably distinct groups. In the context of one market, the effect is felt at the level of income net of signaling costs. Wage discrimination is not a problem in this context.

In a multimarket setting, the effect may be much more profound. For in the multimarket setting, it is possible that employer expectations will be such as to cause entire groups to self-select themselves out of some markets. When this happens, employers' beliefs go unchallenged by market experience and, hence, unaltered. The effect then is a persistent occupational or job separation with an informational underpinning.

The phenomenon need not be based upon a crude set of beliefs that one group is productively less capable than another, although it may be so based. In fact, there may be an interaction with the differential signaling cost phenomenon. In just one market, differential signaling costs do not by themselves lead to discriminatory results. The same is not true in the more realistic multimarket setting. In the multimarket setting, it may be that employers in some industry believe that education means the same thing as a signal, for blacks and whites or men and women. But if education costs more for one group, that group may never appear in the market, and the employers' beliefs are unchallenged. If we were to force some members of the currently excluded group into the market, employers would eventually learn that a given level of education implies more talent for that group, because education costs at given levels of capability are uniformly higher.

A variant occurs when the basis for the differential signaling costs lies in a characteristic which is both unproductive and unobservable. The parents' income case is a possible example. In the one market setting, differential signaling costs with an unobservable source leads to wage discrimination. In the multimarket setting it may produce the effective exclusion of certain potentially productive groups from certain markets. Given the current societal patterns of financial aid to education in the United States, we are more likely to see poor people in business or in academia than in law or medicine, because professional graduate training costs are largely borne by the individual, and the real costs of undertaking it are higher for the less well-to-do.

An analogous phenomenon can, of course, occur, even in the absence of differential signaling costs. Employers may believe that more education is required to signal a given level of competence for some groups than others. This also may lead to the effective exclusion of one or more groups. The only thing differential signaling costs adds is the possibility of effective occupational exclusion even when employers' conditional probabilistic beliefs are formally nondiscriminatory. Employers (and admissions committees, for that matter) may react to certain indices like race when they shouldn't, or when we wish they wouldn't. But they may also fail to react to certain indices when they should.

In general, the lower equilibrium trap in the one market model may turn into gross differences in the patterns of occupational choice in the multimarket setting. Some of these gross differences have a satisfactory explanation in a microeconomic theory with prejudice included.[1] To these it is worth adding the possibility of persistent expectational biases. The analysis suggests these can occur both within markets and across them. There is no reason to expect these mechanisms to be mutually exclusive. On the contrary, they may complement each other.

But they are not the same thing. One way to see this is to ask what kinds of changes can be effected and how the dynamics of change would look. Informationally based job segregation will collapse when the informational system is jarred. The informational barriers are real but fragile. Once the pattern of exclusion is broken, employers' market experiences change, and one might expect a rather rapid "tipping" phenomenon as the system moves quickly to a new equilibrium. On the other hand, barriers based on prejudice are unlikely to disintegrate so rapidly. If the barrier seems to have an informational basis, a simple legislated minimum quota may solve the problem. After it has been operative for a time, it might be possible to remove it with no return to the original equilibrium.[2]

The Absence of Disconforming Evidence for Beliefs

There are many areas in which beliefs are degenerately confirmed because they give rise to behavior which, taken in a suit-

1. See, for example, K. J. Arrow, "Some Models of Racial Discrimination in the Labor Market," RAND Memorandum RM-6253-RC, February 1971; G. Becker, *The Economics of Discrimination* (Chicago: The University of Chicago Press, 1957); T. C. Schelling, "Models of Segregation," RAND Memorandum RM-6014-RC, May 1969; and L. Thurow, *Poverty and Discrimination* (Washington, D.C.: The Brookings Institution, 1969).

2. Note that, in general, the informational equilibria we have been examining are not resilient in the customary fashion. We are accustomed to thinking of market equilibria as price equilibria. If displaced, forces set in to move the system back to where it was. Signaling equilibria are more like putty than rubber. Once displaced, the system settles, with a minimum of fuss, into a new static configuration.

able context, generates no contradictory experience. Self-selection of people out of certain markets is a pervasive class of examples. There may be many others of a related kind. For years, there were no black baseball players in the major leagues. One force for the continuation of this phenomenon was undoubtedly the belief that prejudiced fans would cease attending ball games if blacks were to appear on the roster. As long as all managers believed this, or preferred to believe it, there was very little incentive to conduct the experiment required to disconfirm the belief, especially as it would have been difficult to reverse the experiment. The pattern of entry by blacks into baseball, a trickle that became a flood, suggests that the source of the previous barrier to entry may have been of this informational variety.

The pattern of entry reminds one of a tipping phenomenon.[3] Indeed, one suspects that tipping patterns are partially based on anticipations. If the individual believes at some point that the influx of minority people will continue at least to a point past that individual's threshold level, and if enough other people have the same types of belief, even if their threshold levels differ, then behavior leads to confirmation of the beliefs and the completion of the tipping phenomenon. This can occur even if individual threshold levels are such that, in the absence of anticipatory moving, the tipping in or out would stop.

Moreover, if tipping becomes a regular pattern in societal institutions, that will reinforce people's anticipations of unraveling in new situations. If one has a model in which anticipations or beliefs are important, one has to explain their source. The suggestion here is that tipping in the past provides the data basis for individuals' beliefs about tipping patterns now. These beliefs tend to produce or accelerate tipping in neighborhoods and institutions and these phenomena in turn generate reinforcing data.

It has been observed that arrest rates differ between blacks and whites who are known to have committed criminal acts. The rate is higher for blacks. One factor in this pattern may be

3. Tipping is discussed in detail in T. C. Schelling, "Neighborhood Tipping," Harvard Institute of Economic Research, Discussion paper no. 100, December 1969.

that race is highly observable, and therefore witnesses can remember it. Knowing someone is black narrows the field more than knowing someone is white, purely by virtue of the fact that, in many cases, blacks are a minority.[4]

Another hypothesis is that in the case of classes of crimes for which there are no eyewitnesses, the police may concentrate their efforts on black or poor communities believing, rightly or wrongly, that they are more likely to find the guilty party there. If there is a positive correlation between location of effort and arrests, there will be a bias toward finding criminals in minority groups. Since only data on solved crimes are usable in assessing the proportion of crimes committed by members of various groups, the data will tend to reinforce the initial belief. The equilibrium will depend upon the underlying true proportions and the extent to which location of investigatory effort is correlated with arrests. This element of finding what you are looking for is reminiscent of the job market signaling model. The difference is that here there appears to be no active signaling.

Employer Prejudice

Employer prejudice can produce wage discrimination or occupational exclusion, or both. It may also affect the signaling equilibrium in the market. Consider Table 13.1, a modified version of model 3a in which employers are willing to pay one group only 2/3 of their marginal products.

It is not difficult to see that the equilibria in the market have the familiar form. There are two independent cutoff levels, $\bar{y}_W$ and $\bar{y}_B$. The allowable ranges for these variables are

$$1 < \bar{y}_W < 2,$$

and

$$2/3 < \bar{y}_B < 4/3.$$

4. The mechanism is suggested by David Wheat, "A Consideration of the Disproportionately Large Percentage of Black Arrestees," unpublished paper, November 1971. Mr. Wheat is a teaching and research assistant at the Kennedy School of Government, Harvard University.

Table 13.1. Market Data with Employer Prejudice

Group	Productivity	Employer willing to pay	Education costs
W	1	1	y
W	2	2	$y/2$
B	1	2/3	y
B	2	4/3	$y/2$

The wages and disposable incomes to the various groups in an equilibrium are shown in Table 13.2.

Table 13.2. Outcome of Signaling Game

Group	Productivity	Wages	Education	Disposable income
W	1	1	0	1
W	2	2	$\bar{y}_W$	$2 - \bar{y}_W/2$
B	1	2/3	0	2/3
B	2	4/3	$\bar{y}_B$	$4/3 \, \bar{y}_B/2$

Not only do wages fall, but it is also likely that the level of expenditure on education probably falls in the group discriminated against. In itself, this may not be detrimental. The wage differential is greater than the differences in income after signaling.

Suppose, however, that we were observing this system from the outside. We would observe lower rates of remuneration associated with lower levels of y (say, education) and lower levels of y correlated with Group B. It might then look as if y were productive and people in B suffer because they do not buy or otherwise obtain enough y. The remedy would appear to be to raise the level of y among Group B. In this example, the analysis would be incorrect and the policy ineffective. Raising y would simply raise $\bar{y}_B$.

Statistical Discrimination

The term "statistical discrimination" refers to a situation in which employers draw inferences about productivity from indices, because those indices are correlated with productive capability in the population. Thus size may be an index of strength, because size and strength are correlated. One suspects, although it would be difficult to prove, that when one mentions informational bases for discrimination, most people think in terms of statistical discrimination. How else could a productively irrelevant index be a useful source of information if it is not correlated with anything productively relevant?

I hope to have been convincing in pointing out that as soon as we acknowledge active signaling in the market (education signaling is an example), there are many ways in which indices can be informationally relevant. The statistical discriminatory mechanism is not a misconception, but it is a drastically incomplete view of how indices function in a market information system. And it may not be very important. Recall that many of the equilibria in our models of the interaction of education and race do *not* depend upon the underlying joint distribution of productive capabilities and the index. I would argue, therefore, that the presence of active signaling in most job markets tends to attenuate the force of whatever statistical features there may be in the underlying population.

If productivity is correlated with some index, for whatever reason, the result will be average wage differentials over groups defined by the index. But this has nothing or almost nothing to do with the informational structure of the market. It would be true in a world of perfect information, and it is true in the world where education, by itself, is a perfect signal.

The Misuse of Compensating Categories

Earlier, it was argued that when there are differential signaling costs, failure to adjust for this fact in interpreting active signals leads to discrimination. Unprejudiced employers would tend to compensate, naturally, unless forbidden to do so by the law. Similarly, colleges and graduate schools, while formally denying themselves access to certain indices, informally find it necessary to seek them out. If they do not, they are unable to adjust for previous educational or other disadvantages to blacks or others. And a failure to do so is rightly regarded as discriminatory.

The constitution, however, is color-blind, presumably to protect all people at all times from the adverse effects of certain kinds of prejudice. And the scope of activity deemed to fall within constitutional reach seems to be expanding, over time, at the hands of the courts.[5] Standing on the principle of color blindness, a court recently required the University of Washington Law School to admit a white student whom they had rejected. The student had argued in court that there were several blacks admitted with less impressive qualifications. The court in effect required the law school to uniformly interpret (and apply uniform standards to) all "legitimate" signals.

There are many reasons for worrying about the outcome of the case. Because of past discrimination, there are too few black lawyers, so that the productivity of a black working in a black community is likely to be higher than that of his white counterpart of comparable ability. Second, there are nonappropriable benefits in terms of role models. But the thing which is most worrisome is the failure to distinguish signals from the underlying attributes about which one is really concerned. I can think of no reasonable normative principle which requires the equal treatment of people with the same test scores, or any other index or signal. As we have already seen, equal treatment at the level of social productivity may require unequal treatment at the level of signals.

5. This expansion is associated with an increasingly broad interpretation of "State Action," which is the basis for the application of the 14th Amendment in civil rights cases. There is, of course, in addition to constitutional provisions, civil rights legislation. This legislation also takes a negative form: that race, color, nationality, and so on are no basis for a wide range of economic and social decisions.

However, if the law is to sanction responses of a certain type to indices such as race or sex or family income, it is necessary to be careful. The question is, when is a response to an index justifiable? One might argue that the responder must simply show, on the basis of past experience, that the conditional distribution of capability, given a signal like education, differs over two or more groups. There are at least two things wrong with this argument. First, it *fails* to exclude the kind of differential treatment which results from arbitrary differences in the equilibrium signaling configuration of two or more visibly distinct groups. It is in precisely such cases that suppressing the response to an index is effective in eliminating discriminatory effects.

The second is more difficult to state, but of equal importance. Suppose education costs vary systematically with family income. Race is positively correlated with income. Hence education costs will be positively correlated with race.

It is possible to want to prevent adjustments on the basis of race if the underlying causal factor is poverty. More positively, ideally one wants to allow responses to indices if conditional distributions of capability, given education, vary over groups defined by the index, *and* it is the index itself which is believed to be the underlying determining factor — that is to say, the factor which directly affects signaling costs. There may be several causal factors. Race, sex, and family income may all be relevant. If so, they should all be used.

The more elaborate criterion is harder to apply, since it requires for its application a causal explanation of the sources of educational and other disadvantages. But to fail to use it is to run the risk of introducing further discrimination where it does not now exist. I am not prepared to argue that compensatory interpretation of signals with respect to the wrong indices is worse than no compensatory interpretation at all. I do argue that legally sanctioned responses to indices should aim for the ideal, which is a situation in which responses are to underlying causal factors, whenever these can be identified.

14 Conclusions

In terms of subject matter, the focus of attention, for the most part, has been on situations in which people transmit information about themselves in a marketlike situation. The resulting market signaling games tend to have two distinctive characteristics, not shared by all market signaling games. One is the relatively large number of people in the market at any one time. The other is the relative infrequency with which any one individual appears in the market. These two factors conspire to eliminate investment in signaling credibility by the primary signalers. The benefits are not appropriable.

When signaling takes place, it is on the basis of a very different foundation. Information is transmitted via indices and signals. Indices, which are unalterable (or sometimes unaltered, as in loan markets) observable attributes, are capable of passing statistical information directly. But my primary interest has been in signals. Signals are alterable observable attributes. They function in an informational way when two conditions are met. First, something about the signaler must be unobservable to the receiver of the signals. Whatever this something is, it must affect the way the receiver would prefer to reward or respond to the signaler. And the costs of the signaling activity must be negatively correlated with the unobservable attribute which the receiver values. The only caveat needed here is that, in interpreting specific signaling games, one must not take too narrow a view of either the costs or the rewards. These conditions are to be taken as prerequisites for persistent signaling activities, that is to say, activities whose informational content persists over time.

Market signaling games of this type were examined with the aid of an equilibrium concept. Equilibria are defined in terms of (1) revision of conditional probabilistic beliefs by receivers and (2) a feedback mechanism which generates new data upon which the revision of beliefs is based. The elements in the feedback loop are beliefs generating offered rewards, generating signaling activities, and leading to actual transactions (hiring, in the case of job markets), new market data, and revised beliefs for receivers of signals. An equilibrium is a set of beliefs that need no revision after one cycle. It is to be noted that (1) receivers ultimately learn about the characteristic they could not see before the transaction, (2) beliefs are expressible as conditional probability distributions over the unobserved, given the observed, and (3) the underlying distribution of relevant characteristics in the signaling population is stable over time. This does not mean that the actual people are the same. In job markets they are not. When any of these three conditions fails to hold, the model must be modified. A few examples will serve to illustrate and perhaps to stimulate further research.

With respect to posttransaction informational feedback, there are examples where it is incomplete. One or even several visits to a physician do not supply the layman with all relevant information about the doctor's professional competence. The informational feedback is at best imperfect. With respect to the constancy of the underlying signaling population, one can and should worry about shifts in the composition of the unemployed, job-seeking labor force over a cycle. Academic job markets are currently in a poor state. If this situation persists, one can anticipate shifts in the abilities, interests, and signaling behavior of candidates who appear in these markets in the future. And hiring institutions will have to adapt to the changes.

Signaling equilibria have strange properties by traditional economic standards. There are multiple and often continuous spectra of equilibria. Resiliency is lost. If a signaling equilibrium is exogenously upset, a return to the original equilibrium is at best problematic. Some equilibria are worse than others, in terms of the aggregate consumption of unproductive resources, and sometimes one equilibrium is found to be Pareto inferior to another. The private and social return to education differ when education is a signal. (There are, of course, other reasons why they may differ.) The signaling effect causes the private return to exceed the social. The same conclusions hold for other types of signaling activity: the deliberate acquisition of job experience as a signal for the future is one. The welfare effects of signaling activity are in need of further work, both empirical and conceptual. The empirical question is obvious: by how much do private and social returns differ? Conceptually, to measure welfare losses, we must consider practical alternatives to the current market signaling patterns. Here a great deal of work is required.

Indices interact with signaling. Aside from carrying statistical information (which may or may not be important, depending on the context), indices affect the logical structure of the signaling game by setting natural limits to the informational externalities in the system. Multiple equilibria turn into different equilibria for different groups (as defined by indices). This occurs in both one market and multimarket settings. In the latter, the equilibrium situation may exhibit occupational separation of two or more groups. Indices also affect the signaling game by virtue of being correlated with signaling costs, alternative market opportunities, and sometimes productivity.

Education, job experience, and training are the typical things one thinks of as signals in the context of the job market. Indices are a diverse collection of attributes: test scores, size, sex, race, personal history, criminal record, service record, medical history. Obviously a principal modern public-policy problem, upon which we have only touched here, is that of controlling the storage of, and access to, personal information of this type.[1] In other signaling situations, a variety of signals ranging from conspicuous consumption to the liquidity of one's portfolio can be

1. See, for example, Arthur R. Miller, *The Assault on Privacy* (Ann Arbor: University of Michigan Press, 1971).

found. Indices multiply, and, in some markets (e.g. loans and consumer credit), potential signals such as house ownership become effective indices because the signaling costs swamp the potential gains.

The Need for Further Work on Market Signaling

In the job market paradigm, the single most important determinant of the logical informational structure of the market is the lack of prominence of the primary signalers. They are numerous and appear infrequently in the market on an individual basis. This leads to averaging, externalities, and multiple equilibria. By contrast, consider the large producer and seller of consumer durables. He (or it) has an informational problem. Consumers do not automatically know the quality of a product or even all of its attributes prior to purchasing. There is an informational gap, and hence at least the logical possibility of signaling. But the primary signalers, in this case the large producers and sellers, are (a) relatively few in number and (b) frequently in the market. Indeed they are in the market virtually continuously. One cannot, therefore, expect the informational structure of this kind of market even to approximate that of the job market. The questions, then, are: what does the informational structure of the market look like, and how is information passed, if at all?

I do not have the answers to these questions, nor even a well-formulated model of the relevant features of the situation. But a few considerations or conjectures, based vaguely on having the job market model as a backdrop, may stimulate further effort.

1. Large selling organizations will acquire and maintain signaling reputations. Signaling will in part take the form of various kinds of quality control.

2. Brand names will be important. Consumers are in the market for a particular consumer durable relatively infrequently. Hence cross-product inferences of quality via the brand name are important.

3. As a result, multiproduct sellers, selling under a certain name, will have an informational advantage in the consumer

sector. They will have a competitive advantage and tend to eliminate or absorb single-product firms, even when there are no strictly productive cross-product increasing returns.

4. Multiproduct retail outlets can be expected to have the same type of advantage through cross-product inferences of quality by the consumer. Quality is maintained via the purchasing divisions within the retail firm.

5. Large producers and sellers will invest in projecting an image of generalized technical competence and innovative ability, the benefits of which then accrue to all the products under the company name.

6. One would expect particular producers not to integrate up and down a quality spectrum within their product line, especially when the distinctions between the items in the line are difficult to observe. The reason is that to do so would be to confuse the consumer.

7. Firms will integrate horizontally across products to reap the increasing returns inherent in a generalized reputation for quality products. They will not integrate up and down quality spectra in a particular line. Sometimes they may introduce a new brand name.

8. In terms of multiproduct market organization, one might expect to observe a variety of firms, each horizontally (i.e., product) integrated, and each occupying slightly different places on a *price-quality spectrum,* where price and quality move together. One expects, in other words, quality specialization by firms (or at least brand names).

9. All this depends on the consumer seeing the firm as a coordinated agent and not a loose connection of productive units. Variance in the quality of products under a particular brand name, experienced by the consumer, will destroy the inference and the firms ability to benefit from the increasing returns to a generalized reputation for quality. Hence firms will advertise themselves as purposeful monoliths.

These are conjectures whose validity needs to be tested within the framework of a well-organized set of concepts describing the informational structure of a market. Notice that sellers are selling lotteries. If one thinks of the product as a lottery, then the quality choice for one product will literally alter the other products a firm sells.

Informational Intermediaries

The fact that there may be drastic increasing returns to the collection of information has been noted by many authors. On reflection, the observation suggests the existence of economic organizations whose primary function is to collect and disseminate information of various kinds. But it seems fair to say that, at the present time, our understanding of the services provided, the production functions, and the profitability of such institutions is imperfect or imprecise.

As a first step in this direction, it is well to recognize that there are different kinds of information which can be provided by intermediaries. In the context of job markets, employment agencies can and do centralize the screening process for certain standardized types of jobs. The job market signaling game, as we have described it, is played between applicants and agencies. Agencies then sell the information along with the referral to the ultimate employer. The social return to reducing the number of screening organizations is clear. The profits of the agency come, in part, out of the difference. The agency, of course, communicates with employers on the basis of a conventional signaling code which is maintained because the agency (and the employer), unlike the individual job applicant, is in the market frequently and therefore will rationally invest in its future ability to communicate.

Informational intermediaries do not always pass information only about the uncertain properties of goods and services. There are other kinds of information of value to economic agents: for example, prices, who is in the market, what range of commodities are available. Wholesalers will locate buyers and sellers in a market, pass price information, and even facilitate bargaining over unit prices. All these things are directly observable. From the point of view of economic theory, what is needed is a model that explains or predicts the behavior of such organizations and ultimately sheds some light on (1) the institutions in the market and (2) the efficiency of the market.

The interesting work of Professor R. E. Balderston is worth mentioning here.[2] Imagine m buyers and n sellers on different sides of a market (see Fig. 14.1).

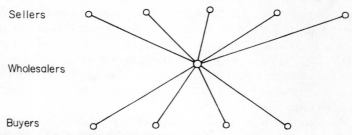

Figure 14.1. A Market Network

Without wholesalers, the number of communication channels required to relay complete price information (which may change over time) is mn. With one informational intermediary, the number drops to $m + n$. With two, the situation is slightly complicated. Assuming sellers are connected to at least one, and buyers to both, the number is $2m + n$. In general, with s wholesalers, the number is $sm + n$. It seems to be true that, on reasonable assumptions about the costs of channels, one intermediary is most efficient. It is by no means clear, however, that we will find one wholesaler in a market equilibrium.

It is not my purpose to attempt an analysis of this situation here. It does seem clear that there are interesting microeconomic problems of this type remaining to be solved.

Price Signaling

Price can be used to signal different things. Some high-priced commodities which are highly visible are signals of status. The

2. F. E. Balderston, oral presentation to summer workshop on Markets and Uncertainty, University of California, Berkeley, summer 1971.

commodity itself is the signal. Its signaling power derives from its high price and the fact that it is known to be high priced. High-fashion designs and exotic cars are examples. The good itself must be either naturally expensive or, in the case of fashion, continually shifting. In either case, the goal is the same: difficulty of imitation.

The market equilibrium in such cases reflects not only the costs of the good, but the implicit congestion phenomenon in the market. As the price rises, some people are driven out of the market. Others stay precisely because the number of buyers is reduced. This is exactly the situation in any typical congestion pricing problem. Therefore, a large part of the price of the good can be attributed to exclusion costs, rather than to production and marketing costs.

Price-status signaling is perhaps less common than price-quality signaling. Price is very often used by sellers, who set the prices, as a direct signal of quality. The seller who is frequently in the market can make prices of goods in a product line correlate with quality. If he does, then price will be taken as a signal of quality by buyers. An immediate question, as yet unsolved, is what is the optimal price-signaling strategy for the monopolistic seller. Only rarely will price be used optimally to convey complete and accurate information. Mixed strategies may sometimes be appropriate, but it is not known when.

When this problem is solved, we can move on to the more difficult question of competitive pricing in situations in which price can, at the discretion of the seller, be used as a signal.

Price-quality signaling systems are examples of conventional signaling systems. They are effective because they are maintained consistently and are learned over time by consumers. As with direct quality choice by a multiproduct seller, there is no reason to expect all sellers to adopt the same price-signaling strategy. On the contrary, one might expect a spectrum of sellers ranging from high average prices and high-quality signaling to lower average prices and much more variance in product quality. This is certainly observable in the range of multiproduct retail outlets found in most large urban areas.

Conventional Signaling Codes

A conventional signaling system is a system in which signalers' choices of signals are made according to rules that stipulate how states of the world are to be related to the appropriate signals. It does not really matter what the signals are, as long as everyone knows the rules and uses them. Languages are conventional signaling systems. "Conventional," in this context, means communicating by convention. We have encountered a few examples with conventional elements. Ski-reporting is an almost pure case of a conventional signaling system. Reports are phoned in by resorts and broadcast on a daily basis. There are virtually no direct signaling costs to the resorts.

As with price-quality signaling, the problem can be attacked in two stages: first, by determining the optimal choice of signaling code by resorts faced with no competitive pressures; and then by examining the effects of competition on the patterns of signaling. Even the first problem is not as easy as it may sound. It can be established that the optimal choice of signaling code involves no mixed strategies; that if skiers have similar preferences and attitudes toward risk, the optimal number of signals is two; that even with dissimilar consumers, the number of signals will remain small and resulting information flows are neither complete nor accurate.

Given the pervasiveness of conventional elements in market signaling games, which are most often neither coordination nor zero sum games, more work needs to be done.

Appendices, Bibliography, Index

Note to Appendices

The appendices concern the job market signaling model. They are intended to extend and generalize the results discussed previously. Specifically, they show that the properties attributed to signaling equilibria do not depend upon the numerical example selected; that multiple equilibria are not the result of a partial equilibrium framework; that employer risk-aversion affects the results, and the risk-averse employer is not driven out of business by the less risk-averse employer; that general signaling equilibria exist; and, finally, that the static general equilibrium model can be extended to cover (1) the fact that a person's signaling and employment history matter, and (2) the fact that individuals take this into account in a forward-looking way in choosing signals and jobs throughout their working lives.

Appendix A. A Continuous, Partial Equilibrium Model of Job Market Signaling

Assumptions and Notation

1. Let

   $n =$ an unobservable unalterable personal characteristic which affects productivity,

   $y =$ an observable, alterable characteristic which may or may not affect productivity,

   $s =$ individual productivity,

   $R(s|y) =$ the employer's conditional distribution over s given y,

   $c(y,n) =$ the cost of signaling y for a person of type n,

   $W_R(y) =$ the employer's offered wage schedule to levels of y, given the conditional distribution $R(s|y)$,

   $A(n) =$ the highest alternative net income outside this market for a person of type n.

2. The employer is risk-neutral, so that

$$W_R(y) = \int s \, dR(s|y). \qquad (1)$$

3. The individual selects y to

$$\max_y \{W_R(y) - c(y,n)\}. \qquad (2)$$

Let

$$\phi_R(n) = \max_y \{W_R(y) - c(y,n)\}. \tag{3}$$

4. Define the set

$$\xi_R = \{n|\phi_R(n) \geq A(n)\}. \tag{4}$$

The set ξ_R is the set of people who stay in this market.
Define:

$$Y_R(n) = \{\bar{y}|W_R(\bar{y}) - c(\bar{y},n) \geq W_R(y) - c(y,n)\}. \tag{5}$$

Define:

$$\Lambda_R = \{y|y \in Y_R(n) \text{ for some } n\}. \tag{6}$$

5. Productivity is determined by n and y according to

$$s = S(n,y). \tag{7}$$

6. Equilibrium is defined as follows. For all $y \in \Lambda_R$ let $R_R^*(s|y)$ be the empirical conditional distribution of s given y which turns up in the sample hired. In an equilibrium, for all $y \in \Lambda_R$

$$R(s|y) = R_R^*(s|y). \tag{8}$$

Proposition 1: If $c_y > 0$, $S_n > 0$, $c_{yn} < 0$, and for some y^* and all y such that if $y \gtrless y^*$, $c_y > s_y$, then there is an equilibrium $R(s|y)$ of the form

$$\begin{aligned} R(s|y) &= 0 &&\text{for } s < f(y) \\ &= 1 &&\text{for } s \geq f(y), \end{aligned}$$

with $f'(y) > 0$.
Proof: If $R(s|y)$ has this form,

$$W_R(y) = f(y), \tag{9}$$

the individual maximizes by setting

$$f'(y) - c_y(y,n) = 0, \tag{10}$$

provided that

$$f''(y) - c_{yy}(y,n) < 0. \tag{11}$$

For those y's which are observed, we required that

$$s = S(n,y) = f(y). \tag{12}$$

Thus (10) and (12) define an equilibrium provided (11) is satisfied. From (10)

$$f'' - c_{yy} - c_{yn}\frac{dn}{dy} = 0. \tag{13}$$

From (10) and (12)

$$\frac{dn}{dy} = \frac{c_y - S_y}{S_n}. \tag{14}$$

Thus

$$f'' - c_{yy} = c_{yn}\left(\frac{c_y - S_y}{S_n}\right). \tag{15}$$

But $c_{yn} < 0, S_n > 0$. Moreover

$$\left.\frac{\partial f'}{\partial f}\right|_{y=y^*} = \frac{c_{yn}}{S_n} < 0. \tag{15.a}$$

Thus by lowering the value of f at y^* we increase f' and hence ensure that all levels of n select $y > y^*$. But then $c_y - S_y > 0$ and the second order condition is satisfied:

$$f'' - c_{yy} < 0. \tag{16}$$

And the second order condition is satisfied. Since $f' = c_y$, the relationship between s and y is one to one, for the observed levels of y. |||

Proposition 2: There is a one parameter family of equilibria under the assumptions of Proposition 1.

Proof: The equilibrium is completely defined by the relations

$$f'(y) = c_y(y,n),$$ (17)

and

$$S(n,y) = f(y).$$ (18)

Eliminating n yields a first order differential equation in $f(y)$, the general solution to which is a one parameter family of curves, all of which are equilibria. |||

Notice that levels of y which are not observed have virtually no influence on the equilibrium. Put another way, if $R(s|\bar{y})$ causes no one to select $y = \bar{y}$, *then* $R(s/\bar{y})$ is an equilibrium conditional distribution for $y = \bar{y}$. No disconfirming data are forthcoming from the market.

The following propositions are devoted to establishing the properties of signaling equilibria.

Proposition 3: As compared with a hypothetical world of perfect information, everyone overinvests in y.

Proof: In a signaling equilibrium,

$$f'(y) = c_y = S_y + S_n \frac{dn}{dy} > S_y.$$ (19)

In a world of perfect information $W'(y) = S_y = c_y$. Hence in the latter, the optimal choice of y is lower.

One wants to compare different equilibria in the market. The equilibrium family will be denoted by $f(y,K)$ where K is the parameter. Let

$$N = S - c = \text{income net of signaling costs.}$$ (20)

Proposition 4: Holding n fixed, $\dfrac{dN}{dK}$ and $\dfrac{ds}{dK}$ have opposite signs. Similarly, $\dfrac{ds}{dK}$ and $\dfrac{dy}{dK}$ have the same signs.

Proof: Differentiating (20) with n fixed we have,

$$\frac{dN}{dK} = \frac{ds}{dK} - c_y \frac{dy}{dK}. \tag{21}$$

Differentiating $s = S(y,n)$ gives

$$\frac{ds}{dK} = S_y \frac{dy}{dK}. \tag{22}$$

Since $S_y > 0$, $\dfrac{ds}{dK}$ and $\dfrac{dy}{dK}$ have the same sign. Substituting in (21) we have

$$\frac{dN}{dK} = \frac{ds}{dK}\left(1 - \frac{c_y}{S_y}\right). \tag{23}$$

Since $c_y > S_y$, $1 - \dfrac{c_y}{S_y} < 0$ and the result is proved. |||

Remark: A shift in the equilibrium which increases either s or y for given n hurts all employees with that n. Conversely, a shift which hurts all employees with given n, increases the level of overinvestment in y for people of that type.

The next proposition argues that shifts in K affect all employees in similar ways. That is to say, if raising K reduces the net income of people with characteristic $\bar{n}$, that it will reduce the net income of everyone.

Proposition 5: If $\dfrac{dN}{dK} < 0$ for any n, then $\dfrac{dN}{dK} < 0$ for all n.

Proof: K can be thought of as fixing the value of $f(v)$ for some fixed value of y. From the equilibrium conditions, with y fixed,

$$\frac{\partial f_y}{\partial f} = \frac{c_{yn}}{S_n} < 0. \tag{24}$$

But solution curves never cross and $f_y > 0$. Hence, all $f(y)$ rise and all $f_y(y)$ fall. Hence for a given level of n, y must be increased to make

$$f_y = c_y(y,n). \tag{25}$$

Therefore, an upward shift in f increases the level of investment in y for all n. From Proposition 4 the net income falls for all levels of N. |||

Remark: Considering employees as a group, shifts in the equilibrium affect everyone the same way. Comparing two equilibria, one will be found to be *Pareto inferior* to the other. Notice, however, that if $S_y > 0$, everyones' productivity will rise or fall, with no change in wages or production costs. This benefit falls generally on society, and is not appropriable by the employees, or only to a very limited extent. And to repeat, the level of investment in education is too high. Its marginal social product falls short of its marginal cost: the private return to education exceeds the social return. In game theory terms, the coalition of all employees would block both Pareto inferior equilibria and all signaling via education.

Proposition 6: The signaling system is destroyed if $c_{yn} > 0$, so that signaling costs are no longer negatively correlated with the characteristic which contributes positively to productivity.

Proof: Suppose $f(y)$ defined an equilibrium. The return to the employee is $N = f(y) - c(y,n)$. From Proposition 1,

$$\frac{d^2N}{\partial y^2} = c_{yn}\left(\frac{c_y - S_y}{S_n}\right) > 0, \tag{26}$$

if $c_{yn} > 0$. Thus the return is a convex function of y, and the optimal choice of y is at the extremes. Hence everyone will set y at its minimum, and there is no effective signaling. |||

Remark: A prerequisite for effective signaling to take place is that signaling costs be negatively correlated with some attribute which positively contributes to productive capability. When, for a particular observable characteristic, this condition is not met, that characteristic cannot be a persistent source of information in an equilibrium.

The reader will note that none of these propositions requires the assumption that $S_y > 0$. In particular, $S_y = 0$ is a possibility, in this case the signal is unproductive. The private return to the signal will be positive and exceed the social return, which is zero. It is even possible that $S_y < 0$, in which case signaling in this market imposes an external cost on the rest of society.

The system is characterized by externalities associated with the fact that one person's signaling decisions affect the market data the employer receives, his conditional probabilistic beliefs, the offered wage schedule, and hence the return to signaling for others. There is no market for these many effects, so that the term "externalities" is appropriate. All the properties attributed to signaling equilibria have their source in this complicated set of externalities.

Finally, it is not necessary to assume that the employer need not observe n, the underlying causal factor determining productivity s. But if the employer does observe n directly, so that his conditional distributions are over n given y, the entire model can be stated in these terms, and the conclusions are not altered at all.[1] The reader can verify that if $n = g(y)$ defines the equilibrium relationship between n and y, the signaling equilibrium is determined by

$$S_n(g,y)g' + S_y(g,y) - c_y(y,g) = 0.$$

The qualitative effects described above can be deduced from this formula.

1. Thomas Schelling drew my attention to this point. I had originally carried the analysis through with n and R $(n|y)$ instead of s. The model was open to the criticism that the employer might not observe what he was required to do in the model.

Appendix B. The Extension of the Partial Equilibrium Model to Include Indices

To the partial equilibrium model we append a variable z, to stand for observable unalterable attributes of individuals, that is to say, indices. The requisite modifications are as follows.

1. Productivity s is, in principle, a function of n, y and z:

$$s = S(n,y,z). \tag{1}$$

2. Signaling costs may depend on z. We write

$$c(n,y,z). \tag{2}$$

3. Employer's conditional distributions depend in principle on y and z, since both are observable. The conditional distribution is denoted

$$R(s \mid y,z). \tag{3}$$

It follows that offered wages depend on y and z, $W_R(y,z)$.

4. Although little use is made of the fact in the partial equilibrium setting, alternative opportunities $A(n,z)$ depend on z as well as n.

Proposition 1: Under these assumptions and with $S_n > 0$, $c_y > 0$, $c_{yn} < 0$, $c_{yy} > 0$, and $S_{yy} < 0$, there is an equilibrium of the form

$$R(s|y,z) = 0 \qquad s < f(y,z)$$
$$\qquad\quad = 1 \qquad s \geq f(y,z), \qquad (4)$$

for some $f(y,z)$. The relations defining the equilibrium f are

$$f_y(y,z) = c_y(y,n,z), \qquad (5)$$

and

$$f(y,z) = S(n,y,z). \qquad (6)$$

Proof: As in A, Proposition 1, for each level of z. Note that z being unalterable is not the subject of individual decisions.

Proposition 2: Even if S, c, and A do not depend on z, f may depend on z, and different groups, as defined by indices, may end up in different signaling equilibrium configurations.

Proof: For each level of z, we can integrate (5) and (6). The result is a one parameter family of curves. Under the assumptions, *the family* corresponding to one level of z will be the same as *the family* corresponding to another. But the member of the family realized in an equilibrium for one z may differ from the member realized for another. In other words, the realized market equilibrium will have the form $f(y,K(z))$, where $K(z)$ determines which member of the equilibrium family is selected for each z. |||

Remark: The multiple equilibria of the previous model become differential signaling equilibrium configurations over groups defined by indices. This is true even if z is irrelevant for productivity, signaling costs, and alternative opportunities.

If the assumption that $S_z = c_z = 0$ is dropped, the equilibrium will be defined by a function $f(y,z,K(z))$, where z is an independent argument.

Proposition 3: If $S_z = c_z = 0$, and if $N = S - c$ is held constant, then $\dfrac{dn}{dz}$ has the sign of $-f_K K'(z)$, provided $c_n < 0$.

Proof: Totally differentiating

$$S - c = \text{constant}, \qquad (7)$$

yields the equation

$$(S_n - c_n)\, dn + (S_y - c_y)\, dy = 0. \tag{8}$$

Totally differentiating

$$f(y,K(z)) = S(n,y), \tag{9}$$

we have

$$S_n\, dn + (S_y - f_y)\, dy - f_K K'(z)\, dz = 0. \tag{10}$$

Eliminating dy and noting that $f_y = c_y$,

$$\frac{dn}{dz} = \frac{f_K K'(z)}{c_n}. \tag{11}$$

If $c_n < 0$, then $\dfrac{dn}{dz}$ has the sign of $-f_z K'(z)$. |||

Remark: The prerequisite for a signaling equilibrium is that $c_{yn} < 0$. This says nothing about c_n. In general, we might expect $c_n < 0$. The opposite would be an unusual case. Note that if $f_K > 0$ for some y, then $f_K > 0$ for all y because of the monotonicity of $f(y,K)$ in y, and the fact that elements in the family do not cross. Thus if $f_K > 0$ and $K'(z) > 0$, then n falls with z for fixed return net of signaling costs. This means productive talent falls for fixed $N = S - c$, as z rises. Groups defined by higher levels of z therefore have the advantage. Conversely, people of equivalent productive capability receive more (net of signaling costs) as z rises. The conclusions, of course, are reversed if $c_n > 0$.

Proposition 4: If $S_z = c_z = 0$, if $N = S - c$ is fixed, if $c_n < 0$ and if $f_K K'(z) > 0$, then $\dfrac{dy}{dz}$ is negative.

Proof: Eliminating dn from (8) and (10) we have

$$\frac{dy}{dz} = \frac{-f_K K'(z)}{(c_y - S_y)}\left(1 - \frac{S_n}{c_n}\right). \tag{12}$$

From previous assumptions $\dfrac{dy}{dz} < 0$. |||

Remark: The assumption that $f_K K'(z) > 0$ amounts to assuming there is an equilibrium expectational bias against lower levels of z. If this situation exists, then people with low levels of z overinvest in the signal to a greater extent, for fixed returns N. If $c_n > 0$, the sign of $\dfrac{dy}{dz}$ is ambiguous.

Thus far, net income has been held fixed. One can also hold wages fixed and examine the effect of the index z from that vantage point. Holding wages constant means setting $S(n,y) =$ constant.

Proposition 5: If $S_z = c_z = 0$, if $f_K K'(z) > 0$ and if $S =$ constant, then

$$\frac{dy}{dz} = \frac{-f_K K'(z)}{c_y} < 0, \qquad (13)$$

and

$$\frac{dn}{dz} = \frac{f_K K'(z)}{S_n c_y} > 0. \qquad (14)$$

Proof: Totally differentiating

$$S = \text{constant} \qquad (15)$$

yields the result

$$S_n \, dn + S_y \, dy = 0. \qquad (16)$$

From (10) we have

$$S_n \, dn + (S_y - f_y) \, dy - f_K K'(z) \, dz = 0. \qquad (17)$$

Eliminating dn and dy in order gives the required result. |||

Remark: Looking only at people with the same wages, and if there is an expectational bias against lower levels of z, then investment in the signal goes down as z goes up, and productive capability goes up with z. In the special case in which $S_y = 0$,

$\dfrac{dn}{dz} = 0$. Everyone receives the same wage at given levels of n. But required investment in the signal is higher for the group in the adverse signaling equilibrium configuration.

Notice that the joint distribution of n and z in the employable population is irrelevant to the signaling equilibrium.

If the assumption that $S_z = c_z = 0$ is dropped, the situation becomes more complicated. There is the direct impact of z and also its influence through the arbitrary parameter. These two effects can be only partially separated.

Proposition 6: If $S_z = 0$ and $c_{yz} < 0$, then if for some $\bar{y}, f(\bar{y},z_1) < f(\bar{y},z_2)$ with $z_1 > z_2$, then $f(y,z_1) < f(y,z_2)$ for all $y > \bar{y}$.

Proof: From the two equilibrium conditions,

$$f_{yz} = c_{yz} + \frac{c_{yn}}{S_n} f_z.$$

If for some y, $f_z = 0$, then $f_{yz} = C_{yz} < 0$. Hence $f(y,z_1)$ can never cross $f(y,z_2)$ from below. Thus, if at some point $\bar{y}$, $f(y,z_1)$ is below $f(y,z_2)$, it will be below for all $y > \bar{y}$. |||

Remark: The effect of the index z on the equilibrium f are pictured in Figure B.1.

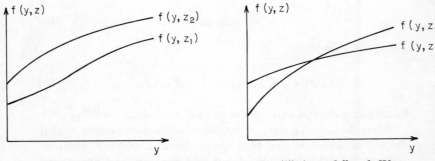

Figure B.1. Possible Effects of z on Equilibrium Offered Wage Schedules

Proposition 7: If $S_z = 0$, $c_{yz} < 0$, then with n fixed,

$$\frac{dN}{dz} = f_z - c_{yz}.$$

Proof: Holding n fixed,

$$\frac{dN}{dz} = (S_y - c_y)\frac{dy}{dz} - c_{yz}.$$

From the equilibrium conditions $f = S$ and $f_y = c_y$,

$$\frac{dy}{dz} = \frac{f_z}{S_y - c_y},$$

so that

$$\frac{dN}{dz} = f_z - c_{yz}.$$

The term $-c_{yz}$ is positive. If f_z is positive for $y = \bar{y}$, $\frac{dN}{dz} > 0$. As n and therefore y increases, f_z falls, so that the magnitude of the gain diminishes unless $-c_{yz}$ increases to compensate. If $f_z = 0$ for $y = \bar{y}$, then $f_z < 0$ for $y > \bar{y}$ and the sign of $\frac{dN}{dz}$ is ambiguous. However, for $y \leq \bar{y}$, $\frac{dN}{dz} > 0$. |||

An important effect of indices is the possibility of differential signaling equilibrium configurations over groups defined by indices. Indices may also affect productivity or they may be correlated with signaling costs. The differential equilibrium effect is then complicated by the direct impacts. The case in which the index affects marginal signaling costs was examined briefly. More detailed study is best done in the context of specific numerical examples of empirical interest. The potential discriminatory effects within the market signaling game are obvious.

Appendix C. The Impact of Employer Risk-Aversion

In this appendix, employer risk-aversion in job market signaling is discussed by means of an example involving a constant absolute risk-aversion utility function. The absence of generality will be noted where appropriate.

Employers are often organizations. The concept of risk-aversion is not, strictly speaking, appropriate. However, in the absence of a theory of organization which predicts behavior as if it were that of a risk-averse individual, it is assumed that risk-aversion in the personnel office is a plausible approximation.

The following proposition allows us to draw some immediate conclusions concerning employer risk-aversion.

Proposition 1: If two individuals have von-Neumann Morgenstern utility indices over money, $u_1(x)$ and $u_2(x)$, and if individual 1 is everywhere more risk-averse, then the certain monetary equivalent of any lottery is less for individual 1 than for individual 2.

Proof: The hypothesis is that

$$-\frac{u''_1(x)}{u'_1(x)} > -\frac{u''_2(x)}{u'_2(x)}. \tag{1}$$

For any $r(x)$, we want to show that

$$u_2^{-1}\left(\int u_2 r \, dx\right) > u_1^{-1}\left(\int u_1 r \, dx\right). \tag{2}$$

Statement (2) holds if and only if

$$u_1 \left(u_2^{-1} \left(\int u_2 r \, dx \right) \right) > \int u_1 r \, dx, \tag{3}$$

if and only if

$$\int \left[u_1 \left(u_2^{-1} \left(\int u_2 r \, dx \right) \right) - u_1 \right] r \, dx > 0, \tag{4}$$

if and only if

$$\int \left[u_1 \left(u_2^{-1} \left(\int u_2 r \, dx \right) \right) - u_1 (u_2^{-1}(u_2)) \right] r \, dx > 0. \tag{5}$$

In Pratt [1964], it is shown that under assumption (1), $f(x) = u_1(u_2^{-1}(x))$ is a concave function of x. Thus, from the definition of concave functions

$$f(u_2(x)) \leq f(\bar{u}_2) + f'(\bar{u}_2)(u_2(x) - \bar{u}_2), \tag{6}$$

where

$$\bar{u}_2 = \int u_2 r \, dx. \tag{7}$$

By rewriting (6), we have

$$f(\bar{u}_2) - f(u_2(x)) \geq -f'(\bar{u}_2)(u_2(x) - \bar{u}_2). \tag{8}$$

Multiplying (8) by $r(x)$ and integrating gives

$$\int [f(\bar{u}_2) - f(u_2(x))] r \, dx \geq 0. \tag{9}$$

But (9) and (4) are the same statements. Hence (2) is true.

The immediate conclusion is that the introduction of employer risk-aversion into a market in which there is uncertainty in an equilibrium lowers everyone's wage. This is true when no active signaling is taking place. When there is signaling, employer risk-aversion may, in addition, change the structure of the signaling equilibrium. The following example is useful, though not perfectly general. It is an extension of the continuous version of model 4.

Notation

n = productivity,
y = the signal,
θy = signaling costs,

(n,θ) are jointly normal with mean[1] $(\bar{n},\bar{\theta})$ and variance-covariance matrix

$$\begin{pmatrix} \sigma_n{}^2 & \sigma_{\theta n} \\ \sigma_{\theta n} & \sigma_\theta{}^2 \end{pmatrix}$$

$-e^{-\lambda n}$ = the employer's utility function over n. It is a constant absolute risk-aversion utility function, where the risk-aversion is the parameter λ.

$W(y)$ = the equilibrium offered wage schedule.

Proposition 2: If X is $n(\mu,\sigma^2)$ and $u(x) = -e^{-\lambda x}$, the certain monetary equivalent (CME) of the lottery corresponding to X is

$$\mu - \frac{\sigma^2\lambda}{2}. \tag{10}$$

Proof:

$$-\int e^{-\lambda x} \frac{1}{\sqrt{2\pi}\sigma} e^{-\frac{1}{2\sigma^2}(x-\mu)^2} \, dx = -e^{-\lambda\left(\mu - \frac{\sigma^2\lambda}{2}\right)} \tag{11}$$

Hence the CME of the lottery is $\mu - \dfrac{\sigma^2\lambda}{2}$. |||

Proposition 3: The conditional distribution of n given θ is normal with mean

1. This is an approximation. We do not want either n or θ to be negative. However, the normality makes the example easier to work with.

$$\bar{n} + \frac{\sigma_{\theta n}}{\sigma_{\theta}^2}(\theta - \bar{\theta}) \tag{12}$$

and variance

$$\sigma_n^2 - \frac{\sigma_{\theta n}^2}{\sigma_{\theta}^2} > 0. \tag{13}$$

Proof: See Pratt et al. [1965]. |||

Proposition 4: The certain monetary equivalent of a lottery on n given θ is

$$\bar{n} + \frac{\sigma_{\theta n}}{\sigma_{\theta}^2}(\theta - \bar{\theta}) + \frac{\lambda}{2}\left(\sigma_n^2 - \frac{\sigma_{\theta n}^2}{\sigma_{\theta}^2}\right). \tag{14}$$

Proof: From Propositions (2) and (3).

Proposition 5: If offered wages are $W(y)$, then the certain monetary equivalent of a lottery on n given y is

$$\bar{n} + \frac{\sigma_{\theta n}}{\sigma_{\theta}^2}(W'(y) - \bar{\theta}) - \frac{\lambda}{2}\left(\sigma_n^2 - \frac{\sigma_{\theta n}^2}{\sigma_{\theta}^2}\right). \tag{15}$$

Proof: If offered wages are $W(y)$, the individual with signaling costs θy will optimize by setting

$$W'(y) = \theta. \tag{16}$$

As a result, the conditional distribution of n given y is normal with mean

$$\bar{n} + \frac{\sigma_{\theta n}}{\sigma_{\theta}^2}(W'(y) - \bar{\theta}), \tag{17}$$

and variance

$$\sigma_n^2 - \frac{\sigma_{\theta n}^2}{\sigma_{\theta}^2}. \tag{18}$$

The conclusion then follows from Proposition (4).

Proposition 6: The one parameter family of equilibrium offered wage schedules $W(y)$ is defined by the differential equation

$$W'(y) + AW(y) = B + \frac{\lambda}{2}\frac{\sigma_\theta^2}{\sigma_{\theta n}}\left(\sigma_n^2 - \frac{\sigma_{\theta n}^2}{\sigma_\theta^2}\right), \tag{19}$$

where

$$A = -\frac{\sigma_\theta^2}{\sigma_{\theta n}} > 0, \tag{20}$$

and

$$B = \bar{\theta} - \bar{n}\frac{\sigma_\theta^2}{\sigma_{\theta n}} > 0, \tag{21}$$

provided that $\sigma_{\theta n} < 0$.

Proof: In equilibrium, $W(y)$ must equal the certain monetary equivalent of the lottery on n given y. Using Proposition (5) the formula follows easily. Note, however, that for $W'(y) = \theta$ to yield an optimum, we require $W''(y) < 0$. Now

$$W''(y) = -AW'(y).$$

Hence we require that $A > 0$ and $W'(y) > 0$ to satisfy the condition. Moreover, $A > 0$ if and only if $\sigma_{\theta n} < 0$. Note that $\sigma_{\theta n} < 0$ means that marginal signaling costs are negatively correlated with productivity. |||

Proposition 7: Let

$$M = -\frac{1}{2}\frac{\sigma_\theta^2}{\sigma_{\theta n}}\left(\sigma_n^2 - \frac{\sigma_{\theta n}}{\sigma_\theta^2}\right) > 0. \tag{22}$$

The equilibrium family of offered wage schedules is

$$W(y,K) = \frac{B - M\lambda}{A} - Ke^{-Ay}, \tag{23}$$

where $K > 0$ is arbitrary.

Proof: By integration of (19). For $W'(y) > 0$, we require $K > 0$. |||

If $\lambda = 0$, the equilibrium offered wage schedule is

$$W(y) = \frac{B}{A} - Ke^{-Ay}. \tag{24}$$

The effect, then, of constant proportional risk-aversion, is simply to reduce all wages by the amount $\frac{M\lambda}{A}$, which depends neither on n or θ. It is linear in λ so that the higher is λ, the larger the reduction. In this example, the optimal choice of y given θ does not depend upon λ. The reason is that $W'(y)$ does not depend on λ. This is the result of the assumption of constant absolute risk-aversion.

The person with unalterable characteristics (n,θ) gets paid

$$\bar{n} + \frac{\sigma_{\theta n}}{\sigma_\theta^2}(\theta - \bar{\theta}) - \frac{\lambda}{2}\left(\sigma_n^2 - \frac{\sigma_{\theta n}^2}{\sigma_\theta^2}\right). \tag{25}$$

Hence wage exceeds productivity if

$$\bar{n} + \frac{\sigma_{\theta n}}{\sigma_\theta^2}(\theta - \bar{\theta}) - \frac{\lambda}{2}\left(\sigma_n^2 - \frac{\sigma_{\theta n}^2}{\sigma_\theta^2}\right) > n. \tag{26}$$

The larger is λ, the fewer the people for whom this is true (see Fig. C.1).

Notice that again there are multiple equilibria, and that increases in K simply increase everyone's investment in y, with no corresponding private or social benefit resulting. Hence the fundamental properties of earlier models are found again here.

One question which naturally suggests itself it whether risk-averse employers are driven out of business by less risk-averse employers. It is not difficult to see that this need not occur. Consider two employers with utility functions of the form $-e^{\lambda_1 n}$ and $-e^{-\lambda_2 n}$, with $\lambda_1 < \lambda_2$. The question is whether everyone will work for the first employer. The answer is not necessarily, even if we exclude the possibility that marginal productivity rises as employment falls in either firm.

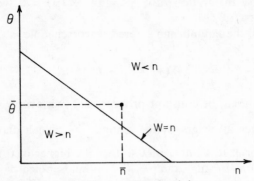

Figure C.1. Relation of Wages to Productivity

To see this, note that the return from working in firm i is

$$\bar{n} + \frac{\sigma_{\theta n}}{\sigma_\theta^2}(\theta - \bar{\theta}) - \frac{\lambda_i}{2}\left(\sigma_n^2 - \frac{\sigma_{\theta n}^2}{\sigma_\theta^2}\right) + \frac{\theta}{\lambda_i}\log\left(\frac{\theta}{K_i A}\right),$$

the last term representing signaling costs. In particular, K_i may not be the same for $i = 1,2$. An individual characterized by (n,θ) therefore chooses firm 1 if

$$\frac{\lambda_1}{2}C + \frac{\theta}{\lambda_1}\log\left(\frac{\theta}{K_1 A}\right) > \frac{\lambda_2}{2}C + \frac{\theta}{\lambda_2}\log\left(\frac{\theta}{K_2 A}\right), \quad (27)$$

where

$$C = \sigma_n^2 - \frac{\sigma_{\theta n}^2}{\sigma_\theta^2} > 0. \quad (28)$$

It is clear that for a given θ, if K_1 is sufficiently large relative to K_2, the individual will choose firm 2. Moreover, if $K_1 > K_2$, we can always find a θ large enough so that the individual will choose firm 2. In general, differential risk-aversion does not necessarily eliminate the more risk-averse employer. However, the more risk-averse employer will get the high signaling cost people, and since signaling cost is negatively correlated with productivity, he will get the less productive people on the average.

Appendix D. Equilibria in Closed Economies

In the partial equilibrium model, there were multiple signaling equilibria, associated with an arbitrary constant of integration, K. One can ask whether this constant is determined, in a multimarket setting, by some interaction in the resource allocation process among markets. The answer is that it is not. Multiple equilibria are not eliminated in this way. The purpose of this section is to demonstrate this fact, by means of a simple model of a closed economy in which job market signaling takes place.

The economy has two sectors. One produces a consumption good using labor. The other produces the signal y, which we may take to be education, also using labor. Signaling takes place in the consumption good industry. Productive capability, n, in the population is distributed according to $g(n)$. The total labor force is

$$L = \int n\, g(n)\, dn.$$

Labor is allocated to the two industries. Thus L_c = the labor employed in the consumption good industry, and L_E is the labor employed in education. The production function for the consumption good is

$$C = L_c^a$$

The production function for education is

$$Y = L_E{}^b.$$

The marginal products of a person with underlying productive capabilities n in the two industries are

$$aL_c{}^{a-1}n,$$

and

$$bL_E{}^{b-1}n.$$

Individuals select signals and industries.

The individual purchases y years of education. The signal s, which is generated, depends on both y and n. The relationship is assumed to be

$$s = ny.$$

The employer in the consumption good industry observes s and infers n. Hence the schedule of offered wages in the consumption good industry depends on s.

Let $f(s)$ be the expected value of n given s in the consumption good industry. Let p be the price of y in terms of the consumption good. Offered wages are

$$aL_c{}^{a-1}f(s),$$

and signaling costs are py. Hence the individual selects y to maximize

$$aL_c{}^{a-1}f(ny) - py,$$

by setting

$$aL_c{}^{a-1}f'(s)n = p.$$

In equilibrium

$$f(s) \equiv n.$$

Hence the equilibrium class of prediction functions $f(s)$ is defined by the equation

$$aL_c^{a-1}f'f = p.$$

Solving for given p and L_c, we have

$$f(s) = \left(\frac{2pL_c}{a}\right)^{1/2}(s - K)^{1/2},$$

where K is an arbitrary constant.

The individual of type n who works in the consumption good industry will set

$$y(n) = \frac{aL_c^{a-1}}{2p}n + \frac{K}{n},$$

and his return net of signaling costs is

$$u(n) = \frac{aL_c^{a-1}}{2}n - \frac{Kp}{n}.$$

These formulae are easily computed using the equilibrium prediction function

$$f(s) = \left(\frac{2pL_c}{a}\right)^{1/2}(s - K)^{1/2}.$$

The individual of type n who works in the education sector does not signal, because his marginal product is assumed to be known. Hence, his wages are his return net of signaling, and these are

$$pbL_E^{b-1}n.$$

The markets must allocate different types of people to different markets. In addition, the labor markets, the education market, and the consumption good market must clear.

An individual of type n will select the consumption good industry if

$$\frac{aL_c^{a-1}}{2} n - \frac{Kp}{n} \geq pbL_E^{b-1}n.$$

Let

$$\phi_c = \left\{ n \Big| \frac{aL_c^{a-1}}{2} n - \frac{Kp}{n} \geq pbL_E^{b-1}n \right\}.$$

The set ϕ_c is the set of people who choose the consumption good industry. Everyone else works in education. It is clear that

$$L_c = \int_{\phi_c} ng(n)\, dn,$$

and that

$$L_E = L - L_c.$$

Now the demand for education is

$$\int_{\phi_c} y(n)g(n)\, dn = \frac{aL_c^{a-1}}{2p} \int_{\phi_c} ng(n) + K \int_{\phi_c} \frac{1}{n} g(n)\, dn$$

$$= \frac{aL_c^a}{2p} + K \int_{\phi_c} \frac{g(n)}{n}\, dn.$$

In equilibrium, this must equal the supply, L_E^b.

Given the conditions for the job markets and the market for education to clear, the fourth and last market, that for the consumption good, clears automatically, by Walras' Law.

To recapitulate, the equilibrium in the model is defined by the following relations.

Total Labor Force Employed

$$(1) \quad L_c + L_E = L = \int ng(n)\, dn.$$

Definition of L_c

$$(2) \quad L_c = \int_{\phi_e} ng(n) \, dn.$$

Choice of Job Market

$$(3) \quad \phi_c = \left\{ n \Big| \frac{aL_c^{a-1}}{2} n - \frac{Kp}{n} \geq pbL_E^{b-1}n \right\}.$$

Education Market Clears

$$(4) \quad L_E^b = \frac{aL_c^{a-1}}{2p} + K \int_{\phi_c} \frac{1}{n} g(n) \, dn.$$

Using these four relationships, it is possible to solve for L_c, L_E, p, and the set ϕ_c. Nothing determines K. In other words, for each K, there is an equilibrium in the closed economy.

Let us look more closely at the set ϕ_c. The relation defining membership is

$$\left(\frac{aL_c^{a-1}}{2} - pbL_E^{b-1} \right) n^2 \geq Kp.$$

Now for given p, let the coefficient of n^2 be

$$M(L_c) = \frac{aL_c^{a-1}}{2} - pbL_E^{b-1},$$

a continuously, monotonically decreasing function of L_c. At $L_c = 0$, $M(0) = +\infty$ and at $L_c = L$, it is $M(L) = -\infty$. It therefore crosses the axis once. Using this fact, one can establish, qualitatively, the pattern of labor allocation in an equilibrium. The set ϕ_c is defined by

$$M(L_c)n^2 \geq Kp.$$

If K is positive, ϕ_c will be empty unless $M > 0$. But ϕ_c cannot be empty in an equilibrium. If it were, an individual's marginal product in the consumption good industry would be $+\infty$. Thus if $K > 0$, $M(L_c) > 0$, and the set of people in the consumption good industry are those for whom

$$n \geq \sqrt{\frac{Kp}{M(L_c)}}.$$

Conversely, if $K < 0$, $M(L_c)$ must be negative and

$$\phi_c = \left\{ n | n \leq \sqrt{\frac{Kp}{-M(L_c)}} \right\}.$$

Notice that the sign of K determines whether the high productivity types work in the consumption sector or the educational sector. If the sign of K changes, there is a complete flip-flop in the pattern of allocation of jobs to people.

There remains the special case when $K = 0$. If $K = 0$, it is easy to see that $M(L_c) = 0$ of necessity. In this case everyone is indifferent between the two sectors. Hence the allocation of labor to the two sectors is largely random. The only condition is that $M(L_c) = 0$ in an equilibrium.

Table D.1 illustrates market equilibrium configurations for different values of K. It was computed under the assumption that n was uniformly distributed on the interval $(1, L - 1)$. In other words

$$g(n) = \frac{1}{L - 2} \text{ on the interval } (1, L - 1)$$

$$= 0 \text{ otherwise.}$$

Most of the relevant characteristics of the signaling equilibria are evident in the table.

The model has a continuum of equilibria dependent upon the arbitrary value of the parameter K. As K rises, L_1 falls and L_2 rises, because increases in K make the first industry relatively less attractive. Similarly, as K rises, p, the price of the signal in terms of the consumption good, falls, because the demand for signals becomes less relative to the supply. For positive values

146 Appendix D

Table D.1. Equilibrium Configurations in the Model

| \multicolumn{4}{c}{Parameters of the system} | \multicolumn{6}{c}{Equilibrium values of the variables*} |
a	b	L	K	L_1	L_2	p	X	U	A_1
1	1	10	7	4.88	5.12	.4818	13.6	13.6	$n \geq X$
1	1	10	3	4.95	5.05	.4919	13.52	13.52	$n \geq X$
1	1	10	1	4.98	5.02	.4972	13.48	13.48	$n \geq X$
1	1	10	−1	5.05	4.95	.5027	13.52	13.52	$n \leq X$
1	1	10	−3	5.14	4.86	.5082	13.64	13.64	$n \leq X$
1	1	10	−7	5.32	4.68	.5189	13.88	13.88	$n \leq X$
.9	.9	10	7	5.1	4.9	.4737	13.31	10.23	$n \geq X$
.9	.9	10	3	5.19	4.81	.4853	13.20	10.15	$n \geq X$
.9	.9	10	1	5.24	4.76	.4915	13.13	10.11	$n \geq X$
.9	.9	10	−1	5.32	4.68	.4970	13.88	10.70	$n \leq X$
.9	.9	10	−3	5.43	4.57	.5014	14.02	10.84	$n \leq X$
.9	.9	10	−7	5.65	4.35	.5096	14.30	11.11	$n \leq X$

* X is defined to the value of n at which the individual is indifferent between the two industries. U is the equilibrium consumption level (stated in terms of y) of the person for whom $n = X$.

of K, it is the higher levels of n who work in the consumption good industry, while the lower levels work in the industry producing y. The conclusion is reversed when K is negative. For people working in the consumption good industry, increases in K damage the lower levels of n (absolutely and relatively) more than the higher levels of n. It is therefore not surprising that as K rises, the lower level n's are driven out of the consumption good industry.

It is useful to consider briefly the welfare implications of changes in K. As we have seen in partial equilibrium models of labor market signaling, lowering K improves the lot of the people working in the first industry. Those who stay are better off. Those who move do so because they are better off in the second industry. Moreover, as K falls, p rises and L_2 falls, so that the marginal revenue product of the person in the second industry who stays there rises. Therefore, he is better off. And if he moves, that indicates an improvement in welfare. Therefore, if

$K_1 < K_2$, the equilibrium configuration corresponding to K_1 is Pareto superior to that corresponding to K_2. It should be emphasized that this feature may be special to the model and not a general property of signaling equilibria. What is true is that, since y is unproductive, or, rather, in any model in which y is unproductive, changes in equilibrium configurations that draw resources away from the unproductive sector increase the total usable product, and, hence, some redistribution of that product will always make everyone better off.

It is possible to show by means of similar examples that multiple equilibria persist in the following cases:

(1) The signal is produced with the consumption good instead of labor;

(2) signaling uses no real resources, only psychic ones;

(3) entirely independent labor forces work in each sector, so that no substitutions are possible;

(4) there is signaling in both sectors;

(5) there are two observably distinct groups defined by observable unalterable characteristics.

Of these, the last seems to be of most interest, since it bears directly upon discriminatory aspects of differential equilibrium signaling configurations over observably distinct groups. The following model captures this case.

It has the same general structure as the previous one. The only difference is that the labor force is divided into two groups on the basis of a dichotomous observable, unalterable characteristic. The groups are referred to as 1 and 2. Each group is divided into two parts in the equilibrium. One part goes to the industry producing the consumption good, and the other goes to the sector producing y. The two industries are referred to as a and b.

Notation

L = the total quantity of labor
L_i = the total supply of labor of type i, $i = 1,2$
L_x = the total quantity of labor in industry x, $x = a,b$

L_{ix} = the amount of labor of type i in industry x
$g_i(n)$ = the distribution of the characteristic n in group i
A_{ix} = the set of n in group i working in industry x, $i = 1,2$; $x = a,b$
$f_x(L_x)$ = the production function for industry x, $x = a,b$.

The following relationships hold among the variables.

$$\sum_{i,x} L_{ix} = L, \qquad (1)$$

$$\sum_{x} L_{ix} = L_i, \qquad (2)$$

$$\sum_{i} L_{ix} = L_x. \qquad (3)$$

The signaling structure of the economy is as before. The signal which the employer receives, s, is a function of n and y,

$$s = ny. \qquad (4)$$

Signaling takes place only in the consumption good industry, $x = a$. In equilibrium, the signals from the two groups may be interpreted differently, and accurately, by the employer in that industry. The equilibrium response of the employer to a person in group i with a signal s is, in terms of the wage paid,

$$f'_a(L_a)T(s), \qquad (5)$$

where the equilibrium point predictor of n for group i is

$$T(s) = \left(\frac{2p}{f'_a(L_a)}\right)^{1/2} (s - K_i)^{1/2}. \qquad (6)$$

It remains to be seen whether the constant of integration K_i is determined in an equilibrium. But, as discussed earlier, these constants are not determined in this particular market, so that K_1 need not equal K_2.

The analysis of the equilibrium is largely the same as the previous model and will only be sketched here. In what follows, it is assumed that

$$f_x(L_x) = L_x^x, \qquad x = a,b. \tag{7}$$

A straightforward calculation shows that a person of type i in industry a with characteristic n has an income net of signaling or consumption level equal to

$$u_{ia}(n) = \left(\frac{aL_a^{a-1}}{2}\right) n - \frac{K_i p}{n}. \tag{8}$$

Individuals of either type in industry b consume their wages (because there is no signaling)

$$u_{ib}(n) = bL_b^{b-1}n, \qquad i = 1,2. \tag{9}$$

The set of people of type i who choose to work in industry a is

$$A_{ia} = \{n | u_{ia}(n) \geq u_{ib}(n)\}, \qquad i = 1,2. \tag{10}$$

And by definition, the quantities L_{ia} are defined by

$$L_{ia} = \int_{A_{ia}} n g_i(n)\, dn, \qquad i = 1,2. \tag{11}$$

The equilibrium system is almost complete. The remaining condition is the market clearing one which is achieved by adjustments in the relative price p. It is

$$L_b{}^b = \frac{aL_a{}^a}{2p} + K_1 \int_{A_{1a}} \frac{g_1(n)}{n}\, dn + K_2 \int_{A_{2a}} \frac{g_2(n)}{n}\, dn. \tag{12}$$

In effect, the equations (10), (11), and (12) determine L_{ia} and A_{ia} for $i = 1,2$ and the price p. All the other quantities are determined by the identities (1) and (2) and (3). Neither K_1 nor K_2 is determined in the equilibrium system. However, they do affect the equilibrium configuration of the economy, as will be seen shortly.

The equilibrium properties of the model are shown in the table of equilibrium configurations, Table D.2. For the purposes

Table D.2. Possible Equilibrium Configurations in the Two-Group Model

K_1	K_2	M	A_{1a}	A_{2a}	A_{1b}	A_{2b}
+	+	+	$n \geq X_1$	$n \geq X_2$	$n \leq X_1$	$n \leq X_2$
+	−	−	empty	$n \geq X_2$	L_1	$n \leq X_2$
+	−	+	$n \geq X_1$	L_2	$n \leq X_1$	empty
−	+	−	$n \leq X_1$	empty	$n \geq X_1$	L_2
−	+	+	L_1	$n \geq X_2$	empty	$n \leq X_2$
−	−	−	$n \leq X_1$	$n \leq X_2$	$n \geq X_1$	$n \geq X_2$

of the calculations, it was assumed that each group is distributed uniformly on the interval $(1, 2L_i - 1)$, $i = 1, 2$. Some points worthy of note are as follows.

(1) There is a double infinity of equilibria associated with the parameters K_1 and K_2.

(2) When $K_i > 0$, the set A_{ia} is defined by an expression of the form

$$n \geqq X_i,$$

and conversely for $K_i < 0$. Thus it is possible to mix the higher level n's of one group with the lower level n's of the other, in either of the two industries.

(3) The lower K_i is, the better off group i is overall. Thus differences in the levels of K_i, which are, from the equilibrium point of view, arbitrary, give rise to what might be called discriminatory situations.

(4) There is, however, no wage discrimination in the model. For an individual is paid an amount proportional to his level of n, in either industry, regardless of which observable group he belongs to. The people who are damaged are the members of the group with the higher K_i, who nevertheless find it profitable to work in the consumption good industry, where, by hypothesis, the signaling takes place. If comparable portions of the n-spectrum in the other group are not present in the same indus-

try, then it may be difficult to draw the comparisons which lead to the conclusion that somewhere, there is discrimination.

(5) By raising K_i enough, it is possible virtually to exclude the ith group from the consumption good industry. Hence, in this way, the model will generate occupational exclusion on the basis of differential employer expectations between the excluded group and others. These expectations concern the meaning of the signals for the various groups.

(6) There is one important difference between this model and the previous one. Suppose that $K_1 > 0$ and $K_2 < 0$. It must be true that the quantity

$$M = \frac{aL_a{}^{a-1}}{2p} - bL_b{}^{b-1}, \tag{13}$$

is either negative or nonnegative. The set A_{ia} is defined by the inequality

$$Mn^2 \geqq K_1, \qquad i = 1,2. \tag{14}$$

Suppose that $M < 0$. Then the set A_{ia} is empty and the first group does not contribute to the labor force in the consumption good industry. On the other hand, if $M > 0$, then

$$Mn^2 \geq K_2 \tag{15}$$

is satisfied for all n, so that everyone in the second group works in the first industry, and no one in the second group is to be found working in the y-sector. Therefore, whenever K_1 and K_2 have opposite signs, at least one group is not found working in one industry. Which group is not found in which industry depends upon both the signs and the magnitudes of K_1 and K_2 (see Table D.2).

It is therefore clear that a wide variety of outcomes is possible in terms of the allocation of the two groups to the two industries. While the model is not intended to approximate any specific pair of markets, it is, I think, suggestive of the rather large potential impacts of signaling phenomena on market allocation procedures.

Appendix E. Allocative and Overall Efficiency and Distributional Considerations in Market Signaling[1]

In many signaling equilibria, information indeed passes to the receiver of the signals. For competitive reasons, such signals will be attended to by potential employers. Wage differentials will reflect this attention. Signaling equilibria are multiple, and some are Pareto inferior to others. The applicability of the Pareto criterion results from the fact that the level of investment in the signal may be reduced without changing the informational content of the signaling system. The conclusion, then, is that some signaling equilibria may be inefficient. There is over-investment in education as compared with a hypothetical world of perfect information. This state of affairs results from the fact that the private return to education (or any other signal) exceeds its direct productivity in an equilibrium.

The question "Are some signaling equilibria inefficient?" has been answered in the affirmative. But the question "Are all equilibria in which signaling takes place inefficient?" has not yet been answered. To answer the second question, one must acknowledge that the information contained in the signals is pro-

1. I have written this largely in response to suggestions and questions raised by Zvi Griliches and George Stigler, to whom I am grateful. On the other hand, since the result of the analysis is, very roughly, that signaling may or may not be worth it, I have placed the analysis in an appendix.

ductive. To this point, the analysis has been confined to situations in which employers used the signals to decide on an offered wage. In such situations, the information contained in the signals is not productive. However, if the employer decides upon both the wage and the job the person is offered, then the information content of the signal may help the employer place the applicant in his area of greatest productivity. Therefore, information can be productive, and one is led to ask the question, "Does the productivity gain resulting from the employer's enhanced capacity to place people in suitable jobs always, usually, or never justify the resource cost of the signaling system?" This is the expanded efficiency question with which this appendix is concerned. To put the matter another way, "Should the signaling system be suppressed or not, and upon what does the answer depend?" [2] If the opportunity for allocating people to "the wrong jobs" on the basis of imperfect information is not explicitly acknowledged, then any signaling is inefficient. Its function is a purely redistributive one. Eliminating signaling activity, in such a world, will simply reduce wage differentials by expanding the sets over which productive capabilities are averaged.

It is clear on reflection that the information content of signals in an equilibrium may affect allocative efficiency on the productive side. Whether or not a signaling system is efficient, therefore, depends upon the relative magnitudes of (a) the signaling costs and (b) the productivity losses that may result from misallocating manpower on the basis of even less perfect information. In this appendix the practice of illustrating points with relatively simple numerical and algebraic examples is continued. Unfortunately, a certain minimal notational complexity, even in these examples, seems unavoidable. The reader is asked to bear with me through a limited amount of plodding detail.

2. It is obvious that any signaling is inefficient when measured against the standard of a world of perfect information. But the world of perfect information is not a very interesting standard. Another possible standard is the world with informational gaps and no signaling. This standard is more interesting because it is potentially achievable (by large increases in signaling costs, for example), and it is the standard I shall use here.

The Elements of a Model

For the time being, it is assumed there are two types of people and one employer. Education is the signal, measured by a continuous scalar index, and is taken to be unproductive. In addition, there are two different types of jobs. Each group (one and two) has a productive capability in each type of job. For the time being, these productivities are taken to be constants.[3] The productivity of a member of group i in job j is denoted f_{ij}.

	Group 1	Group 2
Job 1	f_{11}	f_{21}
Job 2	f_{12}	f_{22}
Education Costs	$a_1 y$	$a_2 y$

Figure E.1. Data on Productivities and Education Costs

In Figure E.1, education costs for group one are given by $a_1 y$ while those for group two are $a_2 y$, both functions being linear for expositional purposes.

The offered wage schedules for each job are denoted by $w_j(y)$ for $j = 1,2$. Notice that there are two of them (as opposed to previous models) and that they depend upon the continuously adjustable, observable signal, y. Finally, the proportion of the population in group one is q_1, and the remainder, $q_2 = 1 - q_1$, is the proportion in group two. That, fortunately, is all the notation that is required.

3. No substantial conceptual adjustment is required to allow for variable marginal products.

Some Assumptions

Thus far, the two groups appear to be symmetrical. It is time to distinguish them by stipulating that some relationships hold among their marginal products. Very roughly, previous convention is followed in making group two the low signaling cost, high-productivity group. A problem about the meaning of high productivity will be resolved shortly.

Assumptions

(1) Signaling Costs
It is assumed that $a_2 < a_1$, the marginal cost of the signal is lower for group two.
(2) Productivities
  (i) $f_{22} > f_{21}$,
  (ii) $f_{22} > f_{11}$, and
  (iii) $f_{11} > f_{12}$.

A word of explanation is in order. The first relationship (i) states that group two is more productive in job 2 than is group two in job 1. In other words, they should be placed in job 2, if productive efficiency is the goal. Relationship (iii) is the converse for group one: they are better placed in job 1. Relationship (ii) states that group two is more productive in its best location than is group one in its best location. In this sense, group two is more productive. The reader may wish to interpret job 2 as the skilled job and job 1 as the relatively less skilled.

In slightly more familiar language, group i has a comparative advantage in job i, $i = 1,2$. In addition, (ii) and (iii) together imply that group two has an absolute advantage in job 2. Who has the absolute advantage in job 1 is important, but unspecified for the moment. One is entitled to ask why this particular set of assumptions. The answer is relatively straightforward. If both groups were most productive in the same job, then the efficiency problem would simply not arise. We could revert to previous models for insights into the impact of signaling.

The second stipulation, $f_{22} > f_{11}$, is a prerequisite for signaling to take place. Therefore, like the assumption on signaling costs, it is best regarded as a signaling prerequisite. That it is truly a prerequisite, will emerge shortly.

The No-Signaling Case

In the absence of signaling (which may be achieved either by fiat, or naturally as an equilibrium), an individual selected randomly from the employable population will have an expected productivity of

$$q_1 f_{11} + q_2 f_{21}, \quad \text{in job 1,} \quad \text{and}$$
$$q_1 f_{12} + q_2 f_{22}, \quad \text{in job 2.}$$

The employer who is optimally allocating employees will place everyone in the job where he has the highest expected marginal product, initially. The wages of everyone are the same,

$$\max (q_1 f_{11} + q_2 f_{21}, q_1 f_{12} + q_2 f_{22}),$$

and everyone goes to the same job. There is a clear efficiency loss here since either one group or the other, is, in the absence of better information, systematically placed in the wrong job. This then is the standard against which various signaling equilibria are to be compared. Notice that with perfect information, average output per worker would be

$$q_1 f_{11} + q_2 f_{22},$$

which is larger than the quantity above. In the one employer model, signaling will always either improve or leave unchanged the productive efficiency of the job allocation process. The main question, then, is whether the efficiency gain exceeds the signaling costs. A second one concerns the distributional effects of signaling. I hope to show that the link between efficiency and signaling costs is tenuous at best.

A Signaling Equilibrium

It seems reasonable to guess that the signal, y, will be used to identify members of the second group, and that these people will be assigned to the second job. The remainder will be placed in the first job. More specifically, the employer's beliefs are hypothesized to have the form:

if $y < \bar{y}$, the person is group one with probability 1, and
if $y \geqslant \bar{y}$, the person is group two with probability 1.

Given these expectations, the employer would like to place people who signal $\bar{y}$ in job 2, and those who signal $y = 0$ in job 1. Now a question which will concern us at several points is how this assignment takes place. For it is at least possible that the individual applicant might refuse his assignment or at least prefer the other job. For the time being, I shall assume that the employer has the freedom to assign people by either refusing to hire the individual for jobs other than the one he wants to place him in, or, almost equivalently, offering to pay him zero on any other job.[4] The offered wage schedules on each job are

4. In the model under consideration, employers are required to pay employees their expected marginal product in the job to which they were assigned. Implicitly offered wages to the job to which they are not assigned are zero. This represents a deviation from the assumption that competitive pressure forces wages to be equal to expected marginal product in all jobs. One can wonder, therefore, whether employer assignment of employees to jobs is compatible with full competitive pressure. My aim here is to show briefly that it is compatible.

In particular, it is easily shown that the following characterizes an equilibrium.

If $y < \bar{y}$, offered wages are f_{11} in job 1 and f_{12} in job 2.
If $y \geqslant \bar{y}$, offered wages are f_{21} in job 1 and f_{22} in job 2.

People in group one rationally select job 1 and those in group two select job 2. The requisite conditions on $\bar{y}$ are as follows.

shown in Figure E.2. People are paid their expected marginal product on the job to which they are assigned.

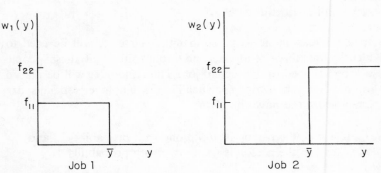

Figure E.2. Offered Wage Schedules

If a person signals $y < \bar{y}$, then, according to the employer's current expectations, he is in group one. His expected productivity in job 1 is f_{11}. His expected productivity in job 2 is f_{12}. The employer ought to know this if he wants, for the sake of efficiency, to place him in job 1. However, offered wages in job 2 are zero

---

Group 1:

$$f_{11} > f_{21} - a_1\bar{y}$$
$$f_{11} > f_{12}, \text{ and}$$
$$f_{11} > f_{22} - a_1\bar{y}.$$

Group 2:

$$f_{22} - a_2\bar{y} > f_{11},$$
$$f_{22} - a_2\bar{y} > f_{21} - a_2\bar{y}, \text{ and}$$
$$f_{22} > f_{12}.$$

Scrutiny of the conditions with the assumptions that $f_{22} > f_{21}$ and $f_{22} > f_{11} > f_{12}$ suggest that the old conditions on y, namely

$$\frac{f_{22} - f_{11}}{a_2} > y > \frac{f_{22} - f_{11}}{a_1}$$

are sufficient here. Hence no violation of competitive pressures in the environment occurs as a result of the assignment assumption, which we use throughout.

for $y < \bar{y}$, and not f_{12}, in order that the correct assignment is assured.

Equilibrium is assured by checking that members of each group optimize by selecting the signals they are expected to select. The signaling cost functions for each group are superimposed on the graphs in Figure E.2. However, the optimizing choices are easier to discern if we collapse the two offered wage schedules into one, as in Figure E.3.

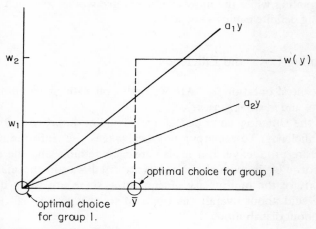

Figure E.3. Signaling Choice

Group one selects $y = 0$, accepts job 1, and is paid f_{11} provided that

$$f_{11} > f_{22} - a_1 \bar{y}.$$

Group two sets $y = \bar{y}$, accepts job 2 and is paid f_{22} provided that

$$f_{22} - a_2 \bar{y} > f_{11}.$$

The critical level $\bar{y}$ will therefore sustain the equilibrium provided that

$$\frac{1}{a_2}(f_{22} - f_{11}) > \bar{y} > \frac{1}{a_1}(f_{22} - f_{11}).$$

Stipulating that $\bar{y}$ must be nonnegative, it is easy to see that $a_2 < a_1$ and $f_{22} > f_{11}$ are both necessary for signaling to take place in an equilibrium of this type: hence, the previous assumptions. As in the simpler models, equilibria are multiple. There is a range of acceptable levels for the signaling parameter, $\bar{y}$. The properties ascribed to previous models apply. However, the multiplicity of welfare nonequivalent equilibria will slightly complicate the discussion of efficiency for the simple reason that the less inefficient signaling equilibria may be better than no signaling while the more inefficient are worse, in which case nothing definite can be said.

Signaling Costs and Efficiency

The central question is, "Are we better off with or without signaling, and in what senses?"

In the situation described above, signaling improves productive efficiency. Total output and total wages rise. Information is therefore productive. But it also costs something, and the costs are borne by individuals in a decentralized way in the market. In spite of the multiplicity of equilibria, there are some things to be said about overall (as opposed to productive) efficiency and about distribution.

Case 1:
Assume that in the absence of signaling *everyone would be allocated to job 1*. In our previous notation, this will occur if

$$q_1 f_{11} + q_2 f_{21} > q_1 f_{12} + q_2 f_{22}.$$

If signaling is introduced, average productivity goes to

$$q_1 f_{11} + q_2 f_{22},$$

or up by the amount

$$q_2(f_{22} - f_{21}),$$

as a result of correctly locating group two to the second job.

Signaling costs go from 0 to $q_2 a_2 \bar{y}$, on the average. Overall efficiency increases if

$$q_2(f_{22} - f_{21}) - q_2 a_2 \bar{y} > 0.$$

This leads to the first result.

Proposition: If, in the absence of signaling, everyone would be assigned to job 1, and if group one has an absolute advantage in job 1 ($f_{21} < f_{11}$), then

(i) group one always benefits from signaling,
(ii) group two always benefits from signaling,
(iii) signaling is more efficient than no signaling.

Proof: It suffices to show that (i) and (ii) hold since (iii) is implied by (i) and (ii). Group one benefits because

$$f_{11} > q_1 f_{11} + q_2 f_{21}$$

under the hypothesis that $f_{11} > f_{21}$ and $q_2 \neq 0$. To show that group two always benefits, it is necessary to show that its members benefit with the worst possible signaling equilibrium. The worst occurs when $\bar{y}$ is near $\frac{1}{a_2} (f_{22} - f_{11})$. In this case, income net of signaling costs is

$$f_{22} - a_2 \cdot \frac{1}{a_2} (f_{22} - f_{11}) = f_{11}.$$

Hence, if $f_{11} > f_{21}$, income net of signaling costs is f_{11} which is greater than the no-signaling wage. |||

To recapitulate, if each group has an absolute advantage in its respective job, signaling benefits all individuals, and is Pareto superior to the no-signaling situation. There remains, of course, a continuum of signaling equilibria which can be ordered in the Pareto manner, because the information content of the signals is being held fixed.

Some of the results can be partially reversed for the case in which $f_{21} > f_{11}$, so that group two has an absolute advantage in both jobs.

Proposition: If everyone would be assigned to job 1 in the absence of signaling, and if $f_{21} > f_{11}$, then

(i) group one is hurt by signaling, and
(ii) group two can be hurt.

Proof: Group one is hurt because

$$f_{11} < q_1 f_{11} + q_2 f_{21}.$$

If the worst signaling equilibrium is achieved, group two individuals also receive f_{11} net of signaling costs and are also hurt. On the other hand, if the best signaling obtains (i.e. $\bar{y}$ is minimized), aggregate output net of signaling costs is

$$q_1 f_{11} + q_2 \left[f_{22} - \frac{a_2}{a_1} (f_{22} - f_{11}) \right].$$

This exceeds average output (wages) without signaling if

$$\left(1 - \frac{a_2}{a_1} \right) f_{22} - f_{21} + \frac{a_2}{a_1} f_{11} > 0.$$

It is easy to see that as $f_{21} \to f_{22}$, the condition above fails to hold. At the other limit as $f_{21} \to f_{11}$, the left hand side becomes

$$\left(1 - \frac{a_2}{a_1} \right) (f_{22} - f_{11}) > 0. \qquad |||$$

Whether signaling *can* improve net productivity in this case, therefore, depends on the size of the absolute advantage group two has in job 1. The larger it is, the less likely is signaling to be useful to group two and to the aggregate. It remains true that some signaling equilibria hurt both groups and hence overall efficiency in the case $f_{21} > f_{11}$.

The level of $\bar{y}$ at which signaling becomes "profitable" for group two (if such a feasible level exists) is above the level of $\bar{y}$ at which signaling becomes efficient relative to no signaling.

Hence it is possible group two would "vote" for signaling even though it is inefficient in the aggregate. Put another way, it is possible that signaling will occur when group two gains, but the system is inefficient in the aggregate.

Case 2:
Let us consider briefly the other case: *the one in which, in the absence of signaling, everyone would be assigned to job 2 by the rational employer.* In the absence of signaling, everyone's wages are

$$q_1 f_{12} + q_2 f_{22}.$$

In this case, it is not possible to state simple conditions under which signaling is efficient. What one can do is relate potential gains and losses to the members of the two groups.

Proposition: If signaling helps group one, then it will also always help group two, and hence be efficient.

Proof: Group 1 is helped if

$$f_{11} > q_1 f_{12} + q_2 f_{22}.$$

Noting that $q_2 = 1 - q_1$, this condition can be written

$$\frac{f_{22} - f_{12}}{f_{22} - f_{11}} > \frac{1}{q_1}.$$

Turning to group two, return net of signaling costs minus the no-signaling wage is

$$f_{22} - a_2 \bar{y} - q_1 f_{12} - q_2 f_{22}.$$

This expression can be rewritten as

$$q_1(f_{22} - f_{12}) - a_2 \bar{y}.$$

The least favorable signaling equilibrium occurs when $\bar{y}$ is at a maximum of

$$\bar{y} = \frac{1}{a_2}(f_{22} - f_{11}).$$

Substituting in the expression above, the group two return net of signaling costs

$$q_1(f_{22} - f_{12}) - (f_{22} - f_{11}).$$

Therefore, group two is better off provided that

$$\frac{f_{22} - f_{12}}{f_{22} - f_{11}} > \frac{1}{q_1}.$$

But if group one is better off, this condition holds. |||

Put in other words, if it is certain that signaling will help group one, then it will help everyone. It is relatively easy to see that if group one is hurt by signaling, group two will be hurt by the least favorable signaling equilibrium. This implies that if group one is hurt, the least favorable signaling equilibrium is inefficient. However, group two may be helped at or near the most favorable equilibrium. The condition for group two to be better off with the most favorable equilibrium is

$$\frac{f_{22} - f_{12}}{f_{22} - f_{11}} > \frac{1}{q_1}\left(q_1 + q_2 \frac{a_2}{a_1}\right).$$

The right hand side is less than $1/q_1$. Hence, it is possible to have an efficient signaling equilibrium even when group one is hurt.

Removing the Expected Value Constraint on Wages

Up to now, it has been assumed that the wage paid to a group of people who have the same relevant observable characteristics must be equal in equilibrium to their average or expected marginal product. Under competitive conditions, this assumption has a certain appeal. However, for investigatory purposes, it is dropped in favor of the hypothesis that the employer need only average out over his entire labor force, and not within each observable group. This freeing up of the wage constraints opens the way for more efficient signaling equilibria, although, as will be seen shortly, this efficiency is purchased with a redistributive effect which may or may not be appealing. The redistributive effect is in the direction of equality of income or wages.

Since wages are not constrained to equal average productivities within jobs, the following notation is required:

w_1 = the wage paid to anyone working in job 1, and,
w_2 = the wage paid to anyone working in job 2.

The employer continues to assign people to jobs, based on the signal. Thus

if $y < \bar{y}$, the person is assigned to job 1 and receives w_1,
if $y \gtrless \bar{y}$, the person is assigned to job 2 and receives w_2.

Group one selects $y = 0$ and goes to job 1, while group two selects $y = \bar{y}$ and enters job 2 (see Fig. E.4).

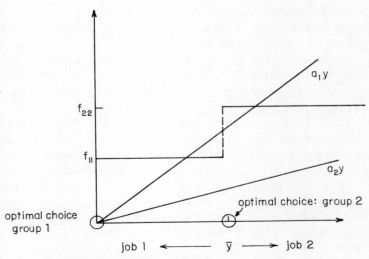

Figure E.4. Job Choice Representation

This, of course, is pictorially the same model as before. However, the wages w_1 and w_2 have acquired some flexibility that was not previously present.

The requisite job choice is made by each group provided that

$$w_1 > w_2 - a_1\bar{y}, \quad \text{and}$$
$$w_2 - a_2\bar{y} > w_1.$$

This translates into the following condition on $\bar{y}$:

$$\frac{1}{a_2}(w_2 - w_1) > \bar{y} > \frac{1}{a_1}(w_2 - w_1).$$

Finally, overall average productivity equals overall average wage if

$$q_1(w_1 - f_{11}) + q_2(w_2 - f_{22}) = 0.$$

The relationship defines the extent of the employer's freedom in setting the wages.

What is striking about this situation is that by reducing the wage differential, one simultaneously lowers the upper and lower bounds of the allowable interval for $\bar{y}$. Of these, the upper bound is more important.

Proposition: The lower the wage differential between the two jobs, the smaller is the maximum per capita expenditure on signaling by members of the second group, in a signaling equilibrium.

The implication is that if wages have the flexibility described above, more efficient signaling equilibria are achievable by collapsing the wage differential and simultaneously reducing the critical level, $\bar{y}$. The equilibria are more efficient, because the information content of the signaling system is unchanged, while the level of investment in the signal is reduced. Signaling costs that are actually incurred can be reduced to arbitrarily low levels by collapsing the wage differential. This yields the following proposition.

Proposition: With wage flexibility, there always exists a signaling equilibrium which is more efficient than the no-signaling situation, provided there is a nontrivial assignment problem facing the employer.

Remaining questions concern the distributional effects of achieving efficient signaling equilibria through manipulation of the offered wages. Since collapsing the wage differential reduces $\bar{y}$, the effect is to reduce the income differential, after signaling costs, of the two groups. Efficiency and equality therefore move together rather than in opposite directions. It is well to remember however, that (a) we are dealing with a highly stylized model, (b) the wage flexibility required may not be present, and (c) the employer has no particularly strong incentive to reduce wage differentials, since the signaling costs are borne by individuals. This is true, even if the wage flexibility is not eliminated by competitive pressures (if the employer is a monopsonist with respect to labor, for example).

Efficiency and distribution questions are most easily examined with the aid of a diagram (Fig. E.5).

On the axes are the incomes net of signaling costs for the two

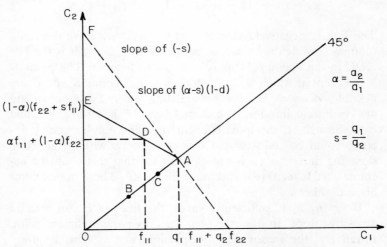

Figure E.5. The Pareto Frontier with Wage Flexibility

groups, denoted by c_1 and c_2. It is assumed that the most favorable signaling equilibrium, given the offered wages, is obtained. It is useful to plot c_2 as a function of c_1, in the wage flexibility case. First, note that

$$c_2 = w_2 - \frac{a_2}{a_1}(w_2 - w_1).$$

Letting $\alpha = \frac{a_2}{a_1}$ and using the fact that $w_1 = c_1$,

$$c_2 = (1 - \alpha)w_2 + \alpha c_1.$$

From the wage break-even constraint,

$$w_2 = f_{22} + \frac{q_1}{q_2}f_{11} - \frac{q_1}{q_2}c_1.$$

Letting $s = \frac{q_1}{q_2}$, the expression for c_2 can be written

$$c_2 = (\alpha - s(1 - \alpha))c_1 + (1 - \alpha)(f_{22} + sf_{11}).$$

The line is negatively sloped if $s(1 - \alpha) > \alpha$. It applies only to areas in which $w_2 > w_1$, or equivalently $c_2 > c_1$. It is the line ADE in the diagram. This is one Pareto frontier. The point D is the point at which $w_2 = f_{22}$ and $w_1 = f_{11}$. Points B and C are possible locations for the no-signaling wage. Such points are always Pareto inferior. The dotted line AF has slope $-s$, and runs through A, the most efficient signaling equilibrium. If income could be redistributed between groups without affecting signaling decisions (it is not clear to me that this could be accomplished), then we could move along AF. These points dominate all others.

If $s = q_1/q_2$ is sufficiently small, the line ADE can acquire a positive slope. In this case, A is the only pareto efficient point. Intuitively, the reason for this phenomenon is that, if group one is sufficiently small, reductions in w_2 are more than compensated for by reductions in signaling costs, so that both groups benefit.

The diagram shows clearly that, with wage flexibility, the no-signaling situation can never be Pareto efficient. There is always a flexible wage signaling equilibrium which dominates it. The point D is that achieved under the most favorable equilibrium if wage flexibility is disallowed. This may or may not dominate the no-signaling situation (in the Pareto sense), depending upon parameter values in the model.

For any pair of wages w_1 and w_2, the least favorable signaling equilibrium is the one in which $\bar{y} = (w_2 - w_1)/a_2$ so that $c_1 = c_2 = w_1$. The locus of these points is simply the $45°$ line, and of course some of these are less efficient than the no-signaling equilibria, which lie on the same locus. In short, signaling can increase efficiency, and, with wage flexibility, equilibria can be found which are Pareto superior to the no-signaling case. But because of the range of indeterminancy in signaling equilibria, efficiency gains are not insured by the mere presence of signaling in the context of wage flexibility.

The Influence of Competition on Signaling

The argument of the last few pages suggests that gains in efficiency are available if wages are freed from the constraint that they equal the expected or average marginal product within groups defined by signals and indices. A natural follow-up question is whether such wage flexibility is compatible with competition in a market in which signaling is also taking place. One can expand the inquiry to ask what are the competitive forces that may act on the signaling system, and what are their implications for efficiency and distribution?

It is important to distinguish two dimensions upon which competitive pressures can operate. One is wages; the other, the level of the signaling prerequisite for entry into the higher productivity job (job 2 in our previous discussion). Since the argument becomes somewhat involved at times, it is useful to outline the conclusions in advance.

1. Signaling itself is not eliminated by competition on either dimension. In fact, firms that fail to use available signals tend to contract the hiring of group two people so as to raise their marginal products and wages to the point where they are competitive with those of firms that are responding to signals.

2. With one qualification, a situation in which wages diverge from marginal products within groups defined by signal levels is not compatible with competition. However, in order to maintain the informativeness of the signal, it is or may be necessary for the competitive firm to raise the signaling prerequisite $\bar{y}$ concurrently with raising wages to group two. Otherwise the employer will find that group one people start signaling $y = \bar{y}$, thereby confusing the signaling system. Since this is a relatively sophisticated move, which might not always be taken by the employer, it is possible that divergence of wages and marginal product may persist. This is the one qualification.

3. Without competition on the signaling dimension, multiple equilibria exist. Wages and signaling prerequisites may differ over firms.

4. Competition along the signaling dimension has several interesting effects. It drives the signaling prerequisite to its lower bound, or near it. It eliminates wage differentials and signaling-prerequisite differentials over similar firms. Wages continue to be tied to average and expected marginal products and multiple signaling equilibria are eliminated. It should hastily be added, that as opposed to wage competition, competing for manpower at fixed wages is not something which the employer has much incentive to do. For signaling costs are borne by the individual. In addition, competing for manpower in the signaling dimension requires a sophisticated understanding of the market environment, and its informational structure.

These points are most easily illustrated by means of a modified version of the model used to examine efficiency. There are two employers instead of one, and marginal products depend upon employment levels. The firms are indexed a and b, with the index appearing as a superscript where appropriate. Each firm has two types of job, and, as before, people are of two types. Signaling costs are the same as in the previous discussion.

Let

$L_{ij}{}^z =$ the number of workers in group i working for z in job j, $(z = a,b)$, and

$Q^z =$ output of firm z.

The production function from firm z is taken to be

$$Q^z = g^z \left(\sum_i f_{i1}{}^z L_{i1}{}^z, \sum_i f_{i2}{}^z L_{y2}{}^z \right).$$

It is assumed that $f_{22}{}^z > f_{21}{}^z$, and that

$$f_{22}{}^z > f_{11}{}^z > f_{12}{}^z, \qquad \text{for each } z.$$

These are the same assumptions as in the one employer model. The marginal product of a member of group i in firm z is

$$m_i{}^z = \max \, [g_1{}^z f_{i1}, g_2{}^z f_{i2}], \tag{1}$$

for $i = 1,2$, where $g_j{}^z$ is the derivative of g^z with respect to its jth argument. Note that $m_i{}^z$ depends upon the numbers of each type in each job within the firm.

Now it is fairly clear that unless the two quantities in the square brackets are equal, all of the members of group i will be in one job or the other, the job in which their marginal product is highest. I shall assume that this is the normal case: that group one always ends up in job 1 and group two in job 2, provided, of course, the signaling system makes them distinguishable. This is done purely for expositional purposes. It can be insured by assuming $f_{12}{}^z = f_{21}{}^z = 0$, for each firm z. Therefore

$$L_{12}{}^z = L_{21}{}^z = 0, \qquad z = a,b. \tag{2}$$

Each employer, z, has a cut off level, $\bar{y}^z$, below which he assumes the person is a member of group one. To complete the model, we require the following variables:

$w_i{}^z =$ is the offered wage to people who are taken to be in group i by firm z,

$L_i =$ the total number of people in group i, and is exogenous to the model.

Everyone is employed eventually, so that

$$L_{ii}{}^a + L_{ii}{}^b = L_i, \qquad i = 1,2. \tag{3}$$

Model 1: Wages Equal Expected Marginal Product for Each Observed Signal

We begin by adopting the wage-equals-marginal-product rule, and assume that there is no competition on the signaling dimension; that is to say, employers do not try to undercut each other's signaling prerequisites for job 2.

The familiar conditions for the signaling equilibrium are

$$w_1{}^z > w_2{}^z - a_1\bar{y}^z, \quad \text{and} \quad \text{(group one sets } y = 0\text{)}$$
$$w_2{}^z - a_2\bar{y}^z > w_1{}^z, \quad \text{(group two sets } y = \bar{y}^z\text{)}$$

for $z = a,b$. More concisely

$$\frac{w_2{}^z - w_1{}^z}{a_2} > \bar{y}^z > \frac{w_2{}^z - w_1{}^z}{a_1}, \tag{4}$$

for $z = a,b$.

In addition

$$w_i{}^z = m_i{}^z(L_{11}{}^z, L_{22}{}^z) \tag{5}$$

for each i and z. This is the wage-equals-marginal-product condition. Finally, in order that members of each group work for both employers, the returns of signaling costs must be the same in each firm. In other words

$$w_1{}^a = w_1{}^b, \quad \text{and}$$
$$w_2{}^a - a_2\bar{y}^a = w_2{}^b - a_2\bar{y}^b. \tag{6}$$

Otherwise one firm would be out of business. It is assumed that marginal products for low input levels are sufficiently high that neither firm will ever go out of business. Essentially, given $\bar{y}^a$ and $\bar{y}^b$, the groups are divided between firms so as to satisfy conditions (6). Using (3) and (5), the equilibrium conditions become

$$m_1^a(L_{11}{}^a, L_{22}{}^a) = m_1^b(L_1 - L_{11}{}^a, L_2 - L_{22}{}^a), \quad \text{and}$$
$$m_2^a(L_{11}{}^a, L_{22}{}^a) - a_2\bar{y}^a = m_2^b(L_1 - L_{11}{}^a, L_2 - L_{22}{}^a) - a_2\bar{y}^b. \tag{7}$$

Given $\bar{y}^a$ and $\bar{y}^b$, these two equations determine $L_{11}{}^a$ and $L_{22}{}^a$, the allocation of labor. Conditions (4) place some restrictions $\bar{y}^a$ and $\bar{y}^b$, but do not determine them. Hence, there are multiple signaling equilibria. Moreover, signaling is not destroyed by competitive pressures at the level of wage competition. The equilibrium conditions map $(\bar{y}^a, \bar{y}^b)$ into sets of possible $(\bar{y}^a, \bar{y}^b)$ pairs. In general, this mapping will have many fixed points, each of which is an equilibrium. Each implies a different allocation of labor between the firms.

Signaling equilibria can persist under competitive pressure, and they will generally be multiple, as before.

Model 2: Flexible Wages and Wage Competition

The social costs of the signaling system can be reduced if wage differentials are reduced. This would imply, of course, that wages differ from marginal products. In the case of group two, wages would be below marginal product, while for group one they would be above. Now the question is whether divergences of wages and marginal products are compatible with competitive firm behavior.

The competitive argument, the reader will recall, is that the employer who finds wages below marginal product for some group will raise wages to expand employment and increase profits. This argument, of course, holds in the signaling situation, but with one important qualification. To see what it is, we refer back to conditions (4). As $w_2{}^z$ is raised, we may find that $(w_2{}^z - w_1{}^z)/a_1 > \bar{y}^z$. If this happens, then group one will start signaling $y = \bar{y}^z$, and the signal will lose its informational content. Two things might happen at that point. The employer might lower w_2^z again. If he does, then wages can get stuck below marginal product. Alternatively, the employer may raise $\bar{y}^z$. To do so would be to exhibit a relatively sophisticated understanding of the signaling environment. In this case (the worst one from the point of view of efficiency), wages will rise to the level of the marginal product.

Wages that deviate from the marginal product will not occur in equilibrium unless, in the course of raising w_2^z (assuming w_2^z starts below marginal product), the employer encounters confusion in the signaling system and, instead of raising $\bar{y}^z$, pulls wages back down. It is interesting to note that an analogous argument starting from the premise that w_2^z exceeds marginal product will show that group two wages can get stuck above marginal product for either employer (or both), unless he is prepared to lower $\bar{y}^z$.

There is a third possibility. One employer, upon encountering confusion in the signals, may simply give up on the signal. If he does, his offered wages to all applicants are the same. In equilibrium, he will find himself with only group one people, provided there is another firm using the signal to distinguish the groups. If operating with only group one is impossible (in the sense of the production function), the firm will revert to heeding the signals or go out of business. Therefore, competitive pressure, far from destroying the signaling system, tends to force employers to pay attention to signals.

Model 3: Competition on the Signaling Dimension

The sophisticated employer, recognizing that individuals are responding not to wages, but rather to returns net of signaling costs, may compete by reducing $\bar{y}^z$ as much as is compatible with maintenance of the informational content of the signal. If this takes place in both firms, signaling prerequisites will be driven down to their lower bounds, as defined by condition (4).

Therefore, competition with respect to $\bar{y}$ increases the efficiency of the signaling system by lowering signaling costs, with no loss of informational content. But it also produces other effects. In fact, it eliminates both wage differentials and signaling prerequisite differentials over firms. The argument is straightforward. As a result of competition on $\bar{y}^z$,

$$\bar{y}^a = \frac{w_z{}^a - w_1}{a_1}, \quad \text{and}$$

$$\bar{y}^b = \frac{w_z{}^b - w_1}{a_1}.$$

But in equilibrium

$$w_2{}^a - a_2 \bar{y}^a = w_2{}^b - a_2 \bar{y}^b.$$

Thus, putting the conditions together, yields

$$\frac{w_2{}^a - w_2{}^b}{a_2} = \bar{y}^a - \bar{y}^b = \frac{w_2{}^a - w_2{}^b}{a_1}.$$

Since $a_2 < a_1$ by assumption, it must be that

$$w_2{}^a = w_2{}^b = w_2$$

and hence that[5]

$$\bar{y}^a = \bar{y}^b = \frac{w_2 - w_1}{a_1}.$$

Therefore, competition on the signal dimension has at least four effects, assuming competitive pressures drive wages to the level of marginal products.

(i) Group two wage differentials are eliminated,
(ii) Signaling prerequisites for job 2 become the same,
(iii) Multiple equilibria are eliminated, and

5. A technical problem occurs if they actually reach their lower bounds, since at that point, group one people become indifferent between setting $y = 0$ and $y = \bar{y}$. This would create confusion in the signaling system.

(iv) Signaling prerequisites are driven to their lowest levels compatible with the signaling system's being informative.

One other point is worthy of attention. From the point of view of the relationship between signaling costs and market equilibrium, the crucial parameter here is a_1, the marginal cost of y to group one. The magnitude of a_2 becomes somewhat irrelevant provided only that it remains below a_1. The policy of lowering a_1, the private marginal signaling costs, can have two effects. If a_2 does not fall and a_1 is lowered enough, the signal will lose its informational content. Short of that point, the social resource cost of signaling will rise, and hence overall efficiency will fall.

Summary

The productivity gains attributable to the information content of market signals may or may not justify the resource cost. Certainly one cannot assume that signaling is more efficient than no-signaling. Whether or not signaling is preferable depends upon the comparative and the absolute advantages of various groups in the various jobs.

The resources absorbed by the signaling system fall as wage differentials between jobs fall. Collapsing wage differentials increases efficiency and redistributes income (net of signaling) in the direction of equality.

Wage competition is compatible with multiple equilibria, but makes wages equal to marginal products. Competition on the signaling spectrum eliminates wage and signaling-prerequisite differentials, forces signaling prerequisites to their lowest levels, and eliminates multiple equilibria.

Appendix F. A General Equilibrium Model of Job Market Signaling

In this section, the existence of signaling equilibria is established in a reasonably general multimarket context.[1]

Assumptions and Notation

1. There are a finite number of firms, a finite number of signals, and a finite number of types of people. People of the same type have the same productive capabilities in all firms and the same signaling costs. This means that two groups may have the same productive characteristics, but different signaling costs, or different productive capabilities but the same signaling costs. Signals can be productive. The finiteness assumption is a mathematical convenience. The numbers could be very large.

2. Within each type, individuals can be allocated to firms and signals according to whatever proportions one desires: groups are infinitely divisible.

3. The proportion of people of type i who signal j and who

1. Kenneth Arrow considerably simplified this proof by pointing out that the correspondence should take $MxT \to P(MxT)$. My original proof had $A:M \to P(M)$. Because of the fact that t_j is ill defined when $m_{ij}{}^z = 0$ for all i, it was necessary to use a limit point of a sequence of fixed points, a clumsy construction. The old proof is sketched in App. G, because it yields more insights into offered wage schedules in an equilibrium.

work for firm z is denoted by $m_{ij}{}^z$. In addition, define the following vectors:

$$m_j{}^z = (m_{1j}{}^z, \ldots, m_{Ij}{}^z),$$
$$m^z = (m_1{}^z, \ldots, m_J{}^z),$$
$$m = (m^1, \ldots, m^Z).$$

By definition

$$m_{ij}{}^z \geq 0, \text{ for all } z, i \text{ and } j,$$

and

$$\sum_{z,j} m_{ij}{}^z = 1, \text{ for all } i.$$

Define

$$M = \{m|\text{satisfying these conditions}\}.$$

4. If firm z knew that a person signaling j was of type i, it would pay him his marginal product, denoted by

$$f_{ij}{}^z(m^z),$$

a continuous function of m^z, the proportions of people of each type employed by the firm. Note that an individual's marginal product depends upon the labor inputs to the firm.

5. The signaling costs are given by

$$c_{ij}{}^z(m) = \text{the cost to a person of type } i$$
$$\text{who works for } z \text{ and signals } j.$$

It is a continuous function of m, the current proportions of people of each type signaling in various ways, working for various firms.

6. The proportion of people of type i in the employable population is q_i. By definition

$$q_i \geq 0,$$

and

$$\sum_i q_i = 1.$$

7. The employer does not observe either type or productivity at the time of hiring; he observes only the signal.

8. The employer z pays t_j^z to a person who signals j. Thus $(t_1^z, \ldots, t_J^z)$ is the offered wage schedule for employer z.

9. Define

$$
\begin{aligned}
t^z &= (t_1^z, \ldots, t_J^z), \\
t &= (t^1, \ldots, t^z), \\
T_j^z &= [\min_{i,m^z} f_{ij}^z(m^z), \max_{i,m^z} f_{ij}^z(m^z)], \\
T &= \underset{z,j}{X} T_j^z.
\end{aligned}
$$

10. An equilibrium is an element $(m,t) \in MxT$ satisfying the following two relations.

(a) Accuracy of Employer Beliefs.

$$
\text{If } m_{ij}^z \neq 0 \text{ for some } i, \ t_j^z = \frac{\sum_i m_{ij}^z q_i f_{ij}^z(m^z)}{\sum_i m_{ij}^z q_i}.
$$

If $m_{ij}^z = 0$, $i = 1, \ldots, I$, $t_j^z \in T_j^z$.

(b) Employee Rationality in Choosing Signals and Firms.

$$
m_{ij}^z = 0 \text{ unless}
$$

$$
t_j^z - c_{ij}^z(m) = \max_{r,s} [t_s^r - c_{is}^r(m)].
$$

Theorem: There exists a signaling equilibrium.

Remark: The proof consists of defining a correspondence on MxT whose fixed points are equilibria, and then showing that the correspondence has at least one fixed point.

Proof:[1] Define $A:MxT \to P(MxT)$ as follows.

$$
(y,W) \in A(m,t) \underset{\text{def.}}{\Longleftrightarrow}
$$

(i) $y \in M$

(ii) $W \in T$

(iii) $y_{ij}^z = 0$ unless $t_j^z - c_{ij}^z(m) = \max_{r,s} [t_s^r - c_{is}^r(m)]$

(iv) If $m_{ij}^z \neq 0$ for some i

$$W_j^z = \frac{\sum_i m_{ij}^z q_i f_{ij}^z(m^z)}{\sum_i m_{ij}^z q_i} \, \epsilon \, T_j^z.$$

Note first that MxT is a compact, convex set, being essentially the Cartesian product of a large number of compact, convex sets.

The next step is to verify that $A(m,t)$ is a compact, convex set. $A(m,t) \subset MxT$ and is therefore bounded. It is closed by definition. Suppose $(y(1),W(1))$ and $(y(2),W(2))$ belong to $A(m,t)$. Let $\alpha \geq 0$, $\beta \geq 0$, and $\alpha + \beta = 1$. The points $(y(1),W(1))$ and $(y(2),W(2))$ are in MxT. Thus

$$\alpha(y(1),W(1)) + \beta(y(2),W(2)) \, \epsilon \, MxT.$$

Suppose $t_j^z - c_{ij}^z(m) < \max\limits_{r,s}[t_s^r - c_{is}^r(m)]$. Then $y_{ij}^z(1) = 0 = y_{ij}^z(2)$. Hence $\alpha y_{ij}^z(1) + \beta y_{ij}^z(2) = 0$, as required. Similarly, if $m_{ij}^z \neq 0$ for some i,

$$W_j^z(1) = W_j^z(2) = \frac{\sum_i m_{ij}^z q_i f_{ij}^z(m^z)}{\sum_i m_{ij}^z q_i}$$

so that

$$\alpha W_j^z(1) + \beta W_j^z(2) = \frac{\sum_i m_{ij}^z q_i f_{ij}^z(m^z)}{\sum_i m_{ij}^z q_i}.$$

Therefore, $A(m,t) \subset MxT$ is compact and convex.

Finally, it is shown that A is an upper semicontinuous correspondence. Assume that $\{(m(v),t(v))\}_{v=1}^{\infty}$ is in MxT with a limit $(\bar{m},t)$, that $(y(v),W(v)) \, \epsilon \, A(m(v),t(v))$ and that $\{(y(v),W(v))\}_{v=1}^{\infty}$ has the limit $(\bar{y},W)$. We want to show that $(\bar{y},\overline{W}) \, \epsilon \, A(\bar{m},t)$.

Clearly $(\bar{y},\overline{W}) \, \epsilon \, MxT$. Moreover, if $\bar{m}_{ij}^z \neq 0$ for some i, then $m_{ij}^z(v) \neq 0$ for v sufficiently large. Hence for v sufficiently large,

$$W_j{}^z(v) = \frac{\sum_i m_{ij}{}^z(v)q_i f_{ij}{}^z(m^z(v))}{\sum_i m_{ij}{}^z(v)q_i}.$$

Taking limits

$$\overline{W}_j{}^z = \frac{\sum_i \overline{m}_{ij}{}^z q_i f_{ij}{}^z(\overline{m}^z)}{\sum_i \overline{m}_{ij}{}^z q_i}.$$

It remains to show that $\bar{y}_{ij}{}^z = 0$ unless

$$\bar{t}_j{}^z - c_{ij}{}^z(\overline{m}) = \max_{r,s} \, [\bar{t}_s{}^r - c_{is}{}^r(\overline{m})].$$

Suppose that $\bar{y}_{ij}{}^z \neq 0$. Since $y_{ij}{}^z(v) \to \bar{y}_{ij}{}^z$, there is a V, such that for all $v \gtrless V$, $y_{ij}{}^z(v) \neq 0$. Because $(y(v),W(v)) \in A(m(v),t(v))$ we have

$$t_j{}^z(v) - c_{ij}{}^z(m(v)) \gtrless t_s{}^r(v) - c_{is}{}^r(m(v)),$$

for all $v \gtrless V$ and all r and s. Taking limits, and using continuity, we have

$$t_j{}^z - c_{ij}{}^z(\overline{m}) \gtrless t_s{}^r - c_{is}{}^r(\overline{m}),$$

for all r and s.

This completes the proof that

$$(\bar{y}, \overline{W}) \in A(\overline{m}, \bar{t}).$$

In summary, the mapping $A:MxT \to \mathcal{P}(MxT)$ is upper semicontinuous, MxT is compact and convex, and all image sets $A(m,t)$ are compact and convex. By the Kakutani fixed point theorem, A has a fixed point, i.e., there is an (m^*,t^*) $\in A(m^*,t^*)$. From the definitions of A and an equilibrium, it is obvious that (m^*,t^*) is an equilibrium of the signaling system.|||

Appendix G. Properties of Signaling Equilibria

We turn now to the properties of job markets signaling equilibria. The first question concerns the offered wage schedule.

Proposition 1: There exists an equilibrium with offered wages $(t_j{}^z)$ with the following properties.

(i) If the signal j is used with respect to firm z, then

$$t_j{}^z = \frac{\sum_i q_i m_{ij}{}^z f_{ij}{}^z(m^z)}{\sum_i q_i m_{ij}{}^z}. \tag{1}$$

(ii) If j is not used and could not rationally be used with respect to firm z, then

$$t_j{}^z = \sum_i q_i f_{ij}{}^z(m^z). \tag{2}$$

(iii) If the signal j is not used but could rationally be used with respect to firm z, then letting

$$T_j{}^z(m) = \{i \,|\, t_j{}^z - c_{ij}{}^z(m) = \max_{r,s}\,[t_s{}^r - c_{is}{}^r(m)]\}, \tag{3}$$

$$t_j{}^z = \sum_{i \in T_j{}^z(m)} r_i f_{ij}{}^z(m^z) \tag{4}$$

where $r_i \geq 0$ and $\sum_{i \in T_j{}^z} r_i = 1$.

Proof: For $\epsilon > 0$, define the mapping $A_\epsilon : M \to M$ as follows

$$y \in A_\epsilon(m) \quad \text{if}$$

(i) $\quad t_j^z = \dfrac{\sum\limits_i q_i(m_{ij}^z + \epsilon) f_{ij}^z(m^z)}{\sum\limits_i q_i(m_{ij}^z + \epsilon)},$ (5)

(ii) $\quad y_{ij}^z = 0$ unless $t_j^z - c_{ij}^z(m) = \max\limits_{r,s}\,[t_s^r - c_{is}^r(m)]$ (6)

(iii) $\quad y \in M$.

It is easy to verify, using an argument analogous to that in App. F, that A_ϵ has a fixed point for any $\epsilon > 0$. Let $\{\epsilon_v\}_{v=1}^\infty$ be a sequence in R with $\epsilon_v > 0$, and $\lim\limits_{V \to \infty} \epsilon_v = 0$. Corresponding to this sequence there is a sequence $\{m(v)\}$ of fixed points of $\{A_{\epsilon_v}\}$. The sequence $\{m(v)\}$ has at least one limit point in M. This limit point is an equilibrium in the signaling game. Call the limit $\bar{m}$. Now consider

$$t_j^z(v) = \frac{\sum\limits_i q_i(m_{ij}^z(v) + \epsilon_v) f_{ij}^z(m^z(v))}{\sum\limits_i q_i(m_{ij}^z(v) + \epsilon_v)}.$$ (7)

If $i \notin T_j^z(\bar{m})$, then $i \notin T_j^z(m(v))$ for all v large enough. Hence $m_{ij}^z(v) = 0$. Thus letting $v \to \infty$ it follows that:

(i) if $\bar{m}_{ij}^z \neq 0$ for some i, condition (i) above is satisfied;

(ii) if $i \notin T_j^z(\bar{m})$ for all i, then

$$\bar{t}_j^z = \sum_i q_i f_{ij}^z(\bar{m}^z),$$ (8)

(iii) if $\bar{m}_{ij}^z = 0$ for all i but $T_j^z(\bar{m}) \neq \phi$, then

$$\bar{t}_j^z = \sum r_i f_{ij}^z(\bar{m}^z),$$ (9)

with $r_i = 0$ for $i \notin T_j^z(\bar{m})$. $|\,|\,|$

Remark: What the proposition shows is that offered wages in an equilibrium are not wildly unreasonable. In fact, they are what one might expect to result from a dynamic process leading to an equilibrium.

184 Appendix G

By way of contrast, one can show that when restrictions on the t_j^z are removed, in particular the requirement that $t_j^z \in [\min_i f_{ij}^z(m^z), \max_i f_{ij}^z)]$, then there is a "no-signaling" equilibrium in which everyone selects the same signal.

Proposition 2: For any signal j, there exists an equilibrium in which everyone selects j.

Proof: Set $t_k^z = -M$ for large M and $k \neq j$. Then $t_k^z - c_{ik}^z(m) < t_j^z - c_{ij}^z(m)$ for all i and k. Everyone selects j, and

$$t_j^z = \sum_i q_i m_{ij}^z f_{ij}^z(m^z) \tag{10}$$

with

$$m_{ij}^z = 0 \quad \text{unless}$$

$$t_j^z - c_{ij}^z(m) = \max_r [t_j^r - c_{ij}^r(m)]. \quad ||| \tag{11}$$

Remark: The monopsonistic firm could take advantage of this fact by forcing everyone to invest in a certain "signal" which was productively profitable to the firm. This would be rational only if some of the gains were appropriable by the firm. The same technique can be used to exclude people from the market. The screening organization must be in a monopsonistic position to do it. Licensing doctors and college teachers with Ph.D.'s are possible examples.

Uncertainty and Stability

From here on, the employer superscript is suppressed and j stands for signal-firm pairs.

Two qualitatively distinct situations are of interest when they are found: there may be *one signal per group,* and there may be *one group per signal.* An equilibrium which has both one group per signal and one signal per group will be called a *pure signaling equilibrium.*

If there is one group per signal, employer uncertainty disappears.

Proposition 3: One group per signal implies that no two groups have the same signaling cost function.

Proof: Suppose that for group i, there is a unique best choice of signal $\sigma(i)$. The assumption is that $\sigma(i) \neq \sigma(s)$ when $i \neq s$. By definition

$$t_{\sigma(i)} - c_{i\sigma(i)} > t_{\sigma(k)} - c_{i\sigma(k)} \tag{12}$$

and

$$t_{\sigma(k)} - c_{k\sigma(k)} > t_{\sigma(i)} - c_{k\sigma(i)}. \tag{13}$$

Adding these inequalities we have

$$c_{i\sigma(i)} - c_{i\sigma(k)} > c_{k\sigma(i)} - c_{k\sigma(k)}. \tag{14}$$

Hence groups i and k cannot have the same signaling cost functions. |||

A more surprising proposition is the following.

Proposition 4: Suppose that signaling cost differentials for two groups are never the same. That is to say, for all groups i and m and signals j and k,

$$c_{ik} - c_{ij} \neq c_{mk} - c_{mj}. \tag{15}$$

Then at most one group will ever be found using a given *pair* of signals.

Proof: Let

$$\Gamma_j(t) = \{i \mid t_j - c_{ij} = \max_r [t_r - c_{ir}]\}. \tag{16}$$

The assertion is that

$$\Gamma_j(t) \cap \Gamma_k(t) \tag{17}$$

contains at most one element, if $j \neq k$. Suppose $i, m \in \Gamma_j(t) \cap \Gamma_k(t)$. Then

$$t_j - c_{ij} = t_k - c_{ik} \tag{18}$$

and

$$t_j - c_{mj} = t_k - c_{mk}. \tag{19}$$

Subtracting (19) from (18) yields

$$c_{mj} - c_{ij} = c_{mk} - c_{ik}, \tag{20}$$

or

$$c_{ik} - c_{ij} = c_{mk} - c_{mj}, \tag{21}$$

contradicting the differential cost assumption. |||

Remark: Differential signaling costs do not guarantee the elimination of uncertainty in equilibrium, but they do set some limits to the dispersion of groups over signals.

Strictly speaking, proposition 4 is more relevant to the question whether there is one signal per group. Differential signaling costs guarantee that two groups will not both split themselves over the same pair of signals.

One signal per group bears on the question of stability. The condition that there is only one rational choice of signal per group will guarantee local stability of the equilibrium. On the other hand, if a group has more than one rational choice, the division of the group over signals is, from the individual's point of view, arbitrary. One might suspect that this would contribute to instability. It is well, however, to be reminded of Samuelson's famous dictum concerning the sense of freedom of movement experienced by the infinitely near-sighted olive at the bottom of a martini glass.

Optimal Signaling

Suppose that groups could be allocated to signals. Let $\Gamma = (\Gamma_1, \ldots, \Gamma_J)$ be a partition of $(1, \ldots, I)$ to signals. The return to the entire population is

$$\sum_j \sum_{i \in \Gamma_j} q_i(t_j - c_{ij}) \tag{22}$$

where

$$t_j = \frac{\sum\limits_{i \in \Gamma_j} q_i f_{ij}}{\sum\limits_{i \in \Gamma_j} q_i}. \tag{23}$$

Substituting for t_j in (22), the return to the entire population is

$$\sum_j \sum_{i \epsilon \Gamma_j} q_i(f_{ij} - c_{ij}). \tag{24}$$

It is clear that (24) is maximized when $i \epsilon \Gamma_j$ only if

$$f_{ij} - c_{ij} \geq f_{ik} - c_{ik} \tag{25}$$

for all k.

Under what conditions will this optimal partition sustain itself as a signaling equilibrium? The following proposition gives a necessary condition.

Proposition 5: If the maximum net return is achievable as an equilibrium, then if $i \epsilon \Gamma_k$

$$f_{ik} - t_k < f_{ij} - t_j, \tag{26}$$

for all $j \neq k$. In other words, the amount by which the individual's marginal product exceeds his wage must be less than the comparable difference for any other signal.

Proof: By construction

$$f_{ik} - c_{ik} > f_{ij} - c_{ij}, \tag{27}$$

for $i \epsilon \Gamma_k$. Suppose that

$$t_k - c_{ik} < t_j - c_{ij}. \tag{28}$$

Then on adding inequalities, we have

$$f_{ik} - t_k > f_{ij} - t_j. \tag{29}$$

Therefore, if the inequality (29) is reversed, it cannot be true that (28) holds. In other words, if $f_{ik} - t_k < f_{ij} - t_j$ for $i \epsilon \Gamma_k$ and $j \neq k$, then the optimum is sustainable as a signaling equilibrium.

Pure Signaling Equilibria

It is difficult to find necessary and sufficient conditions for a pure signaling equilibrium to exist. A set of sufficient conditions is presented below.

Proposition 6: If there exists a renumbering of the signals j and groups i such that

$$\text{(i) } c_{i,j+1} - c_{i,j} > c_{i+1,j+1} - c_{i+1,j} \text{ for all } i \text{ and } j, \tag{30}$$

$$\text{(ii) } f_{ii} - c_{ii} > f_{i+1,i+1} - c_{i,i+1} \text{ for all } i, \tag{31}$$

$$\text{(iii) } f_{ii} - c_{ii} > f_{i-1,i-1} - c_{i,i-1} \text{ for all } i, \tag{32}$$

then there is a pure signaling equilibrium in which group i signals i. That is to say, wages to the signal i are f_{ii} and

$$f_{ii} - c_{ii} > f_{jj} - c_{ij} \tag{33}$$

for all i and j.

Remarks: The three conditions are local conditions, much as the first order conditions are local in the continuous and differentiable models. Conditions (ii) and (iii) say that i is better for group i than $i - 1$ or $i + 1$. Condition (i) says that marginal costs are a decreasing function of the number of the group. It is the analogue of the condition $c_{yn} < 0$ in App. A.

Proof: (1) Condition (i) implies that for $m > i$ and $k > j$

$$c_{mk} - c_{mj} < c_{ik} - c_{ij}. \tag{34}$$

Proof: Using condition (i) repeatedly, we have

$$c_{i,j+1} - c_{ij} > c_{i+1,j+1} - c_{i+1,j} > \cdots > c_{m,j+1} - c_{m,j}. \tag{35}$$

Therefore

$$\begin{aligned} c_{m,j+1} - c_{m,j} &< c_{i,j+1} - c_{i,j} \\ c_{m,j+2} - c_{m,j+1} &< c_{i,j+2} - c_{i,j+1} \\ &\vdots \\ c_{m,k} - c_{m,k-1} &< c_{i,k} - c_{i,k-1}. \end{aligned} \tag{36}$$

Adding these inequalities gives

$$c_{mk} - c_{mj} < c_{ik} - c_{ij} \tag{37}$$

as required.

$$(2) \quad \text{If } j > i, \text{ then } f_{ii} - c_{ii} > f_{jj} - c_{ij}. \tag{38}$$

Proof: From condition (ii), we have

$$\begin{aligned}
f_{ii} - c_{ii} &> f_{i+1,i+1} - c_{i,i+1} \\
f_{i+1,i+1} - c_{i+1,i+1} &> f_{i+1,i+2} - c_{i+1,i+2} \\
&\vdots \\
f_{j-1,j-1} - c_{j-1,j-1} &> f_{j,j} - c_{j-1,j}.
\end{aligned} \tag{39}$$

Adding and rearranging terms yields the inequality

$$f_{ii} - f_{jj} > (c_{ii} - c_{i,i+1}) + (c_{i+1,i+1} - c_{i+1,i+2}) \\
+ \cdots (c_{j-1,j-1} - c_{j-1,j}). \tag{40}$$

Using (34) the last term on the *RHS* can be replaced by

$$c_{j-2,j-1} - c_{j-2,j}. \tag{41}$$

The last term in the series then becomes,

$$c_{j-2,j-2} - c_{j-2,j}. \tag{42}$$

Repeating the process, we conclude that

$$f_{ii} - f_{jj} > c_{ii} - c_{ij}, \tag{43}$$

or

$$f_{ii} - c_{ii} > f_{jj} - c_{ij}. \tag{44}$$

$$(3) \quad \text{If } j < i, f_{ii} - c_{ii} > f_{jj} - c_{ij}.$$

Proof: Analogous to that given for (2) except that we use condition (iii). |||

Adding a constant to the signaling costs of any group i does not affect the signaling equilibrium, a reflection of the fact that only marginal costs matter. Hence, the relationship between productivity and return net of signaling costs is weak, to say the least. However, if some group's optimal signal is cheaper for another group, then the net return to the second group is higher in equilibrium. Suppose $c_{ji} < c_{ii}$. Then we have

$$f_{jj} - c_{jj} > f_{ii} - c_{ji} > f_{ii} - c_{ii}.$$

Appendix H. Dynamics

It is ironic that equilibrium systems are used in economics and elsewhere to avoid the complexity inherent in the dynamics of most ongoing social processes, and that, in order to justify the use of the equilibrium concept, it is necessary to devote some attention to precisely these dynamics. An informational equilibrium system is no exception.[1]

What follows is an attempt to get at the dynamics of adjustment to an informational equilibrium. In the model, employers respond faster than they would in the real world. If anything, this contributes to instability. I have not explicitly built "updating priors" into the model of the adjustment of employers' beliefs. A more comprehensive study of dynamics would contain this element.

Assumptions and Notation

1. Time is divided into discrete periods, indexed by n.
2. Employers offer to pay people who signal j in period n the average marginal product of the people who signaled j and were employed in period $n - 1$.
3. Employees coming onto the labor market in period n re-

1. I have studied the dynamics as a Markov chain. The idea of using this powerful tool comes from Jerry Green, to whom I am grateful.

spond to the data of period n, that is to say, the offered wages by employers in period n. There is no lag here.

4. If some signal j is not used by anyone employed by employer z in period $n - 1$, then z will offer to pay the person who signals j in n exactly what he offered in period $n - 1$ (no experience, no wage offer adjustment).

Under these assumptions, it is intuitively clear that signaling patterns may cycle back and forth, never reaching an equilibrium.

Example 1

In Chapter 3, it was established that if $S(n,y) = n$, and $C(y,n) = y/n$, then the equilibrium employer response functions are

$$f(y) = (2)^{1/2}(y + K)^{1/2}, \tag{1}$$

with K arbitrary. Now suppose that in period n,

$$f_n(y) = (2B)^{1/2}(y + K)^{1/2}, \tag{2}$$

with $B \neq 1$. Then a simple calculation, using the assumptions above, shows that

$$f_{n+1}(y) = (2/B)^{1/2}(y + K)^{1/2}, \tag{3}$$

and that

$$f_{n+2}(y) = (2B)^{1/2}(y + K)^{1/2}. \tag{4}$$

Hence, the employer's expectations cycle around the equilibrium forever. The period of oscillation is two.

Example 2

Suppose there are two groups and two signals. The model is like that of Chapter 3. Each group is $1/2$ of the total population. Let $F = (f_{ij})$ and $C = (c_{ij})$ be the two-by-two matrices of marginal products and costs for the two groups. Let

$$F = \begin{pmatrix} 2.5 & f_{12} \\ 1 & 3 \end{pmatrix} \quad \text{and} \quad C = \begin{pmatrix} .5 & 2 \\ 1 & 2 \end{pmatrix}. \tag{5}$$

Suppose that, initially, $t_1 = 2.5$ and $t_2 = 3$. In this period, both groups will signal one. As a result, in the next period, the employer will set $t_1 = 1.5$ and $t_2 = 2$. In response, group 1 will signal 1 and group 2 will signal 2. This generates the original wage pair $t_1 = 2.5$ and $t_2 = 3$ in the next period, and the cycle begins again.

In the general model it is assumed that there is one firm and a finite number of people of each type. Let

m_{ij} = the number of people of type i signaling j.

The dynamics are viewed as a Markov chain, in which employers behave as described in the assumptions above, but employees make mistakes, or take time to adjust. With the assumption of a finite number of people of each type, the number of possible states of the system in any given period is finite. The system in a given period is described by a vector (t,m), where $t = (t_1, \ldots, t_J)$, the list of offered wages to each signal, and $m = (m_{ij})$, a vector with entries m_{ij} giving the number of people of each type using each signal.

Each t_j can be selected from a finite list of possibilities, generated by the relation

$$t_j = \frac{\sum_i n_{ij} f_{ij}}{\sum_i n_{ij}}, \tag{6}$$

where the n_{ij} take on all possible values, such that at least one n_{ij} for each j is not zero. However, some of the vectors t so generated will never be observed. The ones which might be are those which satisfy the following relations.

There exists an m such that, for each j, if $m_{ij} \neq 0$ for some i, then

$$t_j = \frac{\sum\limits_i m_{ij} f_{ij}}{\sum\limits_i m_{ij}}. \tag{7}$$

Transition Probabilities

The probability of (t,m), given $(\bar{t},\bar{m})$, is denoted by $P(t,m/\bar{t},\bar{m})$. This breaks down into two parts. $P(t/\bar{t},\bar{m})$ is determined by employer behavior as follows.

$P(t/\bar{t},\bar{m}) = 1$ if for all j,
either $\bar{m}_{ij} = 0$ for all i and $t_j = \bar{t}_j$,
or $\bar{m}_{ij} \neq 0$ for some i and $t_j = (\sum\limits_i \bar{m}_{ij} f_{ij})/(\sum\limits_i \bar{m}_{ij})$
$= 0$ otherwise.

$P(m/\bar{t},\bar{m})$ is determined by employee behavior, and

$$P(t,m/\bar{t},\bar{m}) = P(t/t,m)P(m/\bar{t}). \tag{8}$$

Employees are allowed to make mistakes. This can be modeled in many ways. One possibility is as follows. Let $f: R \to R$, be a continuous, strictly decreasing positive function, with $\lim\limits_{x \to \infty} f(x) = 0$. Consider the representative individual of type i confronting the offered wages $\bar{t}$. The probability that he selects signal j is taken to be

$$P_{ij}(\bar{t}) = \frac{f(\max\limits_r (\bar{t}_r - c_{ir}) - \bar{t}_j + c_{ij})}{K_i(\bar{t})}, \tag{9}$$

where

$$K_i(\bar{t}) = \sum_j f(\max\limits_r (\bar{t}_r - c_{ir}) - \bar{t}_j + c_{ij}). \tag{10}$$

Given this assumption, $P(m/\bar{t})$ is generated by building up multinomial distributions.

$$P(m/\bar{t}) = \prod_{i,j} c(m_{i1}, \ldots, m_{iJ}) p_{ij}(t)^{m_{ij}}, \tag{11}$$

where $c(m_{i1}, \ldots, m_{iJ})$ is the number of ways of allocating group i to signals to get the distribution $(m_{i1}, \ldots, m_{iJ})$. In other words, it is coefficient in a multinomial distribution. This completes the description of the Markov chain. Notice that all of the probabilities $P(m/\bar{t})$ are nonzero.

Let the transition matrix be P. It can be shown that P^{J+1} must have positive entries everywhere. In other words, it is possible to get from any state to any other state in at most $J + 1$ steps. The argument is as follows. Starting from any $(\bar{t}, \bar{m})$, any m can be achieved in one step because of employee mistakes. Thereafter, any m has positive probability attached to it. After two steps, t_1 can be set by a suitable choice of m. Thereafter $m_{i1} = 0$ for all i, so as not to disturb t_1. In the third period, t_2 is set in a similar fashion and held. This procedure works until one reaches t_J and period $J + 1$. At that point any t_j can be selected for which there is an m such that (7) is satisfied. But these are all the states in the system.

Since P^{J+1} is strictly positive, the Markov chain is finite, irreducible, and aperiodic. The powerful theorems concerning this type of chain can be utilized.[2] The chain has a unique stationary distribution, q, which satisfies the equations and inequalities,

$$
\begin{aligned}
qP &= q \\
qe &= 1, \text{ and} \\
q &\geq 0,
\end{aligned}
\tag{12}
$$

where e is a vector of 1's of suitable dimension. In the dynamic model, the distribution q may be interpreted as a kind of equilibrium. Starting from any point, the system converges probabilistically (in probability) to this distribution. It remains to discuss the relationship between the stationary distribution and the equilibria found previously in the static models.

First, q does not have the property that $q_i = 0$ if and only if state i is not an equilibrium. In fact, q is strictly positive. To

2. See W. Feller, *Introduction to Probability Theory and Its Applications*, vol. I (New York: John Wiley & Sons, Inc., 1950), and J. G. Kemeny and J. L. Snell, *Finite Markov Chains* (Princeton, N.J.: Van Nostrand, 1960).

see this, suppose that $q_i = 0$. Then from the definition of a stationary distribution,

$$\sum_k q_k P_{ki}{}^{J+1} = 0, \tag{13}$$

which means that every term in the sum is zero, since they are all nonnegative. But all the $P_{ki}{}^{J+1}$ are positive, so that all the q_k must be zero. But this is impossible. Hence q is strictly positive.

There is still the general question of whether most of the stationary probability is concentrated on equilibrium states or not, in this version of the dynamics.

The system with a finite number of individuals of each type may have no equilibrium, it may have one, and it may have many. In all these cases, the stationary distribution exists and is unique. This suggests immediately that the relationship between the stationary distribution and equilibria, when the latter exist, is not perfect. Moreover, even when an equilibrium does exist, the Markov system does not converge in probability to the equilibrium state, as we have just seen. So much for negative results. There is still the question whether, when the probability of suboptimal decisions (i.e., mistakes) by employees is small, the stationary probability attaches most of the probability to equilibria when they exist.

In order to study this question, it is assumed that for each possible t in the system, there is a unique best choice of signal for each group. The generality given up in making this assumption is not serious. Let the maximum probability of error be ϵ/N, where N is the number of states in the system. This can be accomplished by making the function $f(x)$, used in defining transition probabilities, steep enough. The typical row of P will then have one large element and the remaining ones either zero or small (less than ϵ/N). That is to say, for each i, there is a k_i such that $p_{ik_i} > 1 - \epsilon$, and $p_{ij} < \epsilon/n$ for $j \neq k_i$. States of the system can be grouped into the following three types.

1. Those for which $i = k_i$. These are equilibrium states. If error probabilities were zero, they would be absorbing states.

2. There is a collection of minimal sets of states

$E_1, \ldots, E_R$, each with the following property, if $i \, \epsilon \, E_r$, then $k_i \, \epsilon \, E_r$. If error probabilities were zero, then each E_r would be an irreducible and degenerate cyclic subchain.

3. There are states which have the following property. Given state i, there exists a sequence $r_1, \ldots, r_s$ such that $k_i = r_1, k_{r_1} = r_2, \ldots, k_{r_s} = m$, where m is a state of type 1 or 2.

For obvious reasons, one might refer to these types of states as almost absorbing, almost cyclic subchains, and almost transient respectively. All states fall into one of these three categories: the categories are mutually exclusive and exhaustive.

Proposition 1: The stationary probabilities attached to almost transient states can be made arbitrarily small with the size of error probabilities.

Proof: First, we may collapse each E_r into one state which is of type 1, that is, almost absorbing, in the obvious way. Now suppose that for some state i, k_i is of type 1. Then we have

$$q_{k_i} = \sum_s q_s p_{sk_i} \geqq p_{k_ik_i}q_{k_i} + p_{ik_i}q_i. \tag{14}$$

Thus

$$q_i \leqq \frac{q_{k_i}(1 - p_{k_ik_i})}{p_{ik_i}}. \tag{15}$$

But $p_{k_ik_i} > (1 - \epsilon)$, $p_{ik_i} > (1 - \epsilon)$, and $q_{k_i} < 1$, so that

$$q_i < \epsilon/(1 - \epsilon). \tag{16}$$

Thus q_i can be made arbitrarily small by reducing ϵ. This takes care of states which feed type 1 states (or almost cyclic subchains) directly. Now suppose that $q_{k_i} \leqq \epsilon$, for some state i, and $p_{ik_i} > 1 - \epsilon$. Then we have

$$q_{k_i} = \sum_s q_s p_{sk_i} \geq q_i p_{ik_i}. \tag{17}$$

Therefore, noting that $q_{k_i} \leq \epsilon$, and $p_{ik_i} > 1 - \epsilon$, we have

$$q_i < \epsilon/(1 - \epsilon). \tag{18}$$

Hence any state which feeds type 1 states indirectly can be made arbitrarily small with the error probabilities. Since all type three states feed absorbing states or chains either directly or indirectly, all can be made arbitrarily small with the error probabilities. |||

The conclusion, then, is that the dynamic system has a stationary distribution in which the highest probabilities attach either to equilibria or to cyclic patterns which are closed. Without additional assumptions it is not possible to go further than this. It is not true that the cyclic patterns have low probabilities attached to them, as the following simple example shows.

$$P = \begin{pmatrix} 1 - \epsilon & \epsilon/2 & \epsilon/2 \\ \epsilon/2 & \epsilon/2 & 1 - \epsilon \\ \epsilon/2 & 1 - \epsilon & \epsilon/2 \end{pmatrix}. \qquad (19)$$

The stationary distribution is $q_1 = q_2 = q_3 = 1/3$. Thus the probability of being in the almost cyclic subset consisting of states 2 and 3 is $2/3$.

Although this is not an attractive possibility from the point of view of equilibrium analysis, it is not without interest in itself. The signaling system may go into an irreducible, finite state cycling pattern and stay there with a high probability, even when errors permit the system to get out of the cycle. Notice that such a closed cyclic subchain can be regarded as a regularized sequence of occupational tipping phenomena. Groups tip in and out of occupations and signal classes, as the externalities implicit in the averaging procedure continually overtake them.

Up to this point, use has not been made of the fact that the transition matrix has a certain amount of structure associated with the large number of zeros which it contains. Let the sequence (t^v, m^v), $v = 1, \ldots, V$, be the states in a cycle. The cycle is depicted in Figure H.1.

If (t^*, m^*) are an equilibrium pair, then none of the t^v can be equal to t^*, because if they were that would stop the cycle. In pictorial terms t^* generates itself (see Fig. H.2).

Hence no equilibrium set of offered wages ever appears in a cycle.

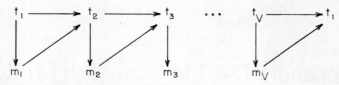

Figure H.1. Interaction in a Chain

Figure H.2. Interaction in an Equilibrium

Although cycles can be complicated, there is a pattern to them. Suppose that group i switches from signal j to signal k between steps v and $v + r$. Then excluding inequalities, we have

$$t_k{}^{v+r} - c_{ik} > t_j{}^{v+r} - c_{ij} \qquad (20)$$

and

$$t_j{}^v - c_{ij} > t_k{}^v - c_{ik}.$$

Adding the inequalities yields

$$t_k{}^{v+r} - t_k{}^v > t_j{}^{v+r} - t_j{}^v. \qquad (21)$$

This has nothing to do with group i. If some other group switched in the opposite direction, then the opposite inequality could be deduced yielding a contradiction. Hence the following proposition.

Proposition 2: Between any two distinct periods in a cycle, it is not possible to find that two groups simply change places with respect to choice of signal.

Appendix I. A Flow-through Model of Signaling and Job Choice: A Generalization of the Static Signaling Model

The equilibrium model discussed in Appendix F is essentially a static model. It therefore omits a number of intertemporal aspects of signaling decisions in the job market context. The important intertemporal aspects of the problem can be identified and then incorporated into an intertemporal equilibrium signaling model. The resulting model is referred to as a flow-through model, to suggest that successive waves of people pass through the system making forward-looking choices with respect to both signals and jobs. The distinction between signals (like education) and jobs, in this context, will naturally be blurred.

In developing the flow-through model, I want not only to incorporate the intertemporal aspects of the signaling game, but also to secure the foundations of the less general static model, by showing that it can be regarded as a time slice of the flow-through model.

Facts

1. After a person has worked for an employer, that employer may know more about his productive capabilities than anyone else. The employer may fire the individual, adjust his wages, or change his job. The individual may resign and seek employment elsewhere. When he does this, his work history is part of his visi-

ble image. It is, viewed retrospectively, an index. The employee is, in effect, a new lottery to future employers.

2. Individuals know that their work histories become signals, and they make their choices of signals and jobs in a forward-looking manner with this fact in mind.

3. Some signals are "irreversible." It is difficult, if not impossible, for example, to divest oneself of a college education.

4. In the intertemporal context, it becomes important for employees to predict their productive capabilities at various types of jobs. The reason is that their performance on any given job will become a future signal and either open or close employment opportunities. Selecting a job is itself a signaling decision, and the outcome of the decision is uncertain. Moreover, the employee loses his relative anonymity with respect to firms for whom he works. Since there are obvious advantages in escaping from being viewed as the average, it is important to select carefully the employers who will know him better.

These, then, are some of the elements of the job market signaling game which the static model cannot encompass, because it does not keep track of individual's histories.

Assumptions and Notation

1. There are N periods or logical stages in a person's working life. The exact timing of these is not important. At the end of each period, employers and employees make new decisions. A signaling game develops. Some people switch jobs. Others stay where they are. Staying where one is is assumed to be a decision.

2. By period n, an individual has acquired a history, consisting of three parts. The first is a list of employers $(z_1, \ldots, z_n)$, denoted by Z_n. The second is a list of signals $(j_1, \ldots, j_n)$, denoted by J_n. The third is a list of evaluations by previous employers $(x_1, \ldots, x_n)$, denoted by X_n. I shall discuss these evaluations later.

3. There are a finite number of individuals, firms, and signals. The proportion of people of type i is $q_i \geq 0$, with $\sum_i q_i = 1$.

4. Let $f_i(Z_n,J_n) =$ the productivity of an individual of type i working for z_n having signaling j_n, and with partial history (Z_{n-1},J_{n-1}).

5. Let $m_i(Z_n,J_n,X_{n-1}) =$ the proportion of people of type i with history $(Z_{n-1},J_{n-1},X_{n-1})$, working for z_n having signaled j_n.

The following relations hold.

$$m_i(Z_n,J_n,X_{n-1}) \geq 0,$$

$$\sum_{z_n,j_n,x_{n-1}} m_i(Z_n,J_n,X_{n-1}) = m_i(Z_{n-1},J_{n-1},X_{n-2}),$$

$$\sum_{Z_n,J_n,X_{n-1}} m_i(Z_n,J_n,X_{n-1}) = 1.$$

6. Signaling costs depend on histories. Let $c_i(Z_n,J_n,X_{n-1}) =$ the cost to a person of type i of signaling j_n and working for z_n, given the history $(Z_{n-1},J_{n-1},X_{n-1})$. If j_n is impossible given $(Z_{n-1},J_{n-1},X_{n-1})$, we take $c_i(Z_n,J_n,X_{n-1}) = +\infty$, thereby allowing for irreversibility in signaling. Note that in so defining costs, tastes for jobs and signaling activities may depend on jobs held and previous signaling activity.

7. Let $t_i(Z_n,J_n,X_{n-1}) =$ the wage offered by firm z_n to a person of type i, given the current signal j_n and the history $(Z_{n-1},J_{n-1},X_{n-1})$.

8. If someone has worked for an employer in the past, it is assumed that the employer knows his productive capabilities. Hence:

if $z_m = z_n$ for some $m < n$, then
$$t_i(Z_n,J_n,X_{n-1}) = f_i(Z_n,J_n).$$

9. Let $t(Z_n,J_n,X_{n-1}) =$ the z_nth employer's expectation concerning the productivity of a person who has signaled j_n and has history $(Z_{n-1},J_{n-1},X_{n-1})$. It is assumed that

if $z_m \neq z_n$ for all $m < n$, then
$$t_i(Z_n,J_n,X_{n-1}) = t(Z_n,J_n,X_{n-1}).$$

10. It is necessary to account for the source of the $t(Z_n, J_n, X_{n-1})$. The assumption is:

if $m_i(Z_n, J_n, X_{n-1}) \neq 0$ for some i, then

$$t(Z_n, J_n, X_{n-1}) = \frac{\sum_i q_i m_i(Z_n, J_n, X_{n-1}) f_i(Z_n, J_n)}{\sum_i q_i m_i(Z_n, J_n, X_{n-1})},$$

if $m_i(Z_n, J_n, X_{n-1}) = 0$ for all i, then

$$\min_i f_i(Z_n, J_n) \leq t(Z_n, J_n, X_{n-1}) \leq \max_i f_i(Z_n, J_n).$$

11. It is assumed that x_n, the employer evaluation, can take on only two values: above or below average.[1] Each employer makes these reports at the end of each period. They become part of a person's record. It is further assumed that employers make mistakes. Specifically, let $h:R \to R$ be monotonic, non-decreasing, and continuous with $h(-\infty) = 0$ and $h(+\infty) = 1$. Then

$h[f_i(Z_n, J_n) - t(Z_n, J_n, X_{n-1})] =$ the probability that a person of type i with (Z_n, J_n) whose productivity is $f_i(Z_n, J_n)$ is reported above average when the employer's expectation is $t(Z_n, J_n, X_{n-1})$.

By manipulating h, we can make the probability of error as small as we like, or make the employer biased in either direction. An example is depicted in Figure I.1.

In the example, reducing ϵ reduces the scope for error. If the report is above average, then $x_n = a$. Otherwise, $x_n = b$.

12. Let $p(x_n | Z_n, J_n, X_{n-1}) =$ the expected proportion of people working for z_n, having signaled j_n, with histories $(Z_{n-1}, J_{n-1}, X_{n-1})$ who receive an evaluation of x_n at the end of period n.

---

1. This assumption is purely for expositional clarity. Any finite scoring of employees by employers would do just as well.

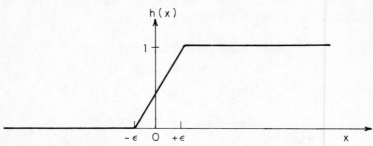

Figure I.1. The Function $h(x)$

The employee will use these proportions to estimate his employment record prospectively. These probabilities are constrained to be accurate if there is any data.

if $m_i(Z_n, J_n, X_{n-1}) \neq 0$ for some i, then

$$p(a|Z_n, J_n, X_{n-1}) = \frac{\sum_i q_i m_i(Z_n, J_n, X_{n-1}) h[f_i(Z_n, J_n) - t(Z_n, J_n, X_{n-1})]}{\sum_i q_i m_i(Z_n, J_n, X_{n-1})}$$

if $m_i(Z_n, J_n, X_{n-1}) = 0$ for all i, then

$$p(a|Z_n, J_n, X_{n-1}) \, \epsilon \, [0,1].$$

13. Employees select pairs (z_n, j_n) in each period. To do this intelligently, they must anticipate future earnings and future decisions. The problem is that there is not much data available on which to base these anticipations. While it seems reasonable to assume an individual correctly predicts signaling costs, it is not reasonable to assume he can predict his productivity and hence his evaluations. The individual does not know his type, since that would, by definition, be equivalent to knowing his productive capability on any conceivable job. Data on offered wages would be helpful, but such data are not public information. Data on actual employment and wage patterns are public, but these are the result of individual optimizing decisions as well as wage offers, and hence are not terribly informative with respect to prospective wage offers.

My suggestion, therefore, is that the individual tends to fall back on a second-order principle. It is that his predecessors have, by and large, made rational decisions, and that he is likely to proceed through the system along paths with probabilities equal to the proportions of people who have gone through it in the past. In this way the individual will estimate his expected earnings in the future. He will subtract the expected signaling costs, using these same proportions, and arrive at a figure for expected future net earnings. To make this precise, let

$S_i(Z_{n-1}, J_{n-1}, X_{n-1})$ = the expected future net return from n to N of a person of type i with history $(Z_{n-1}, J_{n-1}, X_{n-1})$. It depends on i only because signaling costs depend on i.

It is assumed that

(i) if $m_k(Z_n, J_n, X_{n-1}) \neq 0$ for some k and (z_n, j_n), then

$$S_i(Z_{n-1}, J_{n-1}, X_{n-1}) = \sum_{z_n, j_n, k} d_k(Z_n, J_n, X_{n-1}) \{ t_k(Z_n, J_n, X_{n-1})$$
$$- c_i(Z_n, J_n, X_{n-1}) + h[f_i(Z_n, J_n)$$
$$+ t(Z_n, J_n, X_{n-1})][S_i(Z_n, J_n, (X_{n-1}, a))]$$
$$- S_i(Z_n, J_n, (X_{n-1}, b))] + S_i(Z_n, J_n, (X_{n-1}, b))\},$$

where

$$d_k(Z_n, J_n, X_{n-1}) = \frac{q_k m_k(Z_n, J_n, X_{n-1})}{\sum_{s, z_n, j_n} q_s m_s(Z_n, J_n, X_{n-1})}.$$

(ii) If $m_k(Z_n, J_n, X_{n-1}) = 0$ for all k and (z_n, j_n), then $S_i(Z_{n-1}, J_{n-1}, X_{n-1})$ takes on any value in the closed interval bounded by its minimum and maximum values.

In spite of the visual complexity of these relationships, all that is being asserted is that the S_i's are defined recursively as the expected future wages minus expected signaling costs, where the probabilities attached to each possible future path are equal to the proportions of people on each in the past.

14. The individual is assumed to maximize the sum of his

net return in the current period and his expected net return after that. Thus the person of type i with history $(Z_{n-1}, J_{n-1}, X_{n-1})$ will

$$\max_{z_n, j_n} [t_i(Z_n, J_n, X_{n-1}) - c_i(Z_n, J_n, X_{n-1})$$
$$+ p(a|Z_n, J_n, X_{n-1})S_i(Z_n, J_n, (X_{n-1}, a))$$
$$+ p(b|Z_n, J_n, X_{n-1})S_i(Z_n, J_n, (X_{n-1}, b))].$$

Operationally this means that

$$m_i((Z_{n-1}, \bar{z}_n), (J_{n-1}, \bar{j}_n), X_{n-1}) = 0 \text{ unless}$$

$(\bar{z}_n, \bar{j}_n)$ maximizes the expression in square brackets above.

There is no need to define an equilibrium. The definition is contained in the assumptions. The equilibrium is achieved when all expectations are supported by available data, whenever such data exist. This means that t, S, and p are accurate, and that m is generated by appropriate employee decisions. The variables in the model may be represented by the vector (t, m, p, S). As compared with the static model, the new variables are the $t_i(Z_n, J_n, X_{n-1})$ and the p and S. The t_i enter because an employer knows about employees who have worked for him previously. The p and S enter because employees anticipate employer evaluations and future earnings. The flow of interrelationships in the equilibrium model is depicted in Figure I.2. An arrow is to be read as "determines."

Figure I.2. Equilibrium Relationships in the Flow-through Model

Note that, formally, this is an equilibrium model of lifetime employment decisions and the accumulation of human capital, and not just signaling, though it also includes the possibility of signaling via one's accumulated history.

Theorem: There exists an equilibrium in the flow-through model.

Remark: The proof offered below is a sketch. It differs insignificantly from the proof in the static case.

Proof: The correspondence will be denoted by A. It is clear that the variables t, t_i, p, and S_i lie in closed intervals whose Cartesian product is a compact convex set. Similarly, the m_i lie in a linear subspace intersected with nonnegative orthant. This set is also compact and convex. Hence the variables of the model lie in a compact convex set in Euclidean space of high but finite dimension. The correspondence A maps this set into subsets of itself. The correspondence A is defined using the equilibrium conditions as follows:

$$(w, y, r, U) \in A(t, m, p, S),$$

if and only if,

(1) (a) $w_i(Z_n, J_n, X_{n-1}) = w(Z_n, J_n, X_{n-1})$ if $z_m \neq z_n$ for all $m < n$.

    (b) $w_i(Z_n, J_n, X_{n-1}) = f_i(Z_n, J_n)$ if $z_m = z_n$ for some $m < n$.

(2) If $m_i(Z_n, J_n, X_{n-1}) \neq 0$ for some i, then

    (a) $w(Z_n, J_n, X_{n-1}) = \dfrac{\sum\limits_i q_i m_i(Z_n, J_n, X_{n-1}) f_i(Z_n, J_n)}{\sum\limits_i q_i m_i(Z_n, J_n, X_{n-1})}$

    (b) $r(a|Z_n, J_n, X_{n-1})$

$$= \frac{\sum\limits_i q_i m_i(Z_n, J_n, X_{n-1}) h(f_i(Z_n, J_n) - t(Z_n, J_n, X_{n-1}))}{\sum\limits_i q_i m_i(Z_n, J_n, X_{n-1})}$$

(3) If $m_i(Z_n, J_n, X_{n-1}) = 0$ for all i, then

    (a) $w(Z_n, J_n, X_{n-1}) \in [\min\limits_i f_i(Z_n, J_n), \ \max\limits_i f_i(Z_n, J_n)]$

    (b) $r(a|Z_n, J_n, X_{n-1}) \in [0,1]$

(4) $y_i((Z_{n-1}, \bar{z}_n), (J_{n-1}, \bar{j}_n), X_{n-1}) = 0$ unless $(\bar{z}_n, \bar{j}_n)$ maximizes

$$t_i(Z_n, J_n, X_{n-1}) - C_i(Z_n, J_n, X_{n-1})$$
$$+ p(a|Z_n, J_n, X_{n-1}) S_i(Z_n, J_n, (X_{n-1}, a))$$
$$+ p(b|Z_n, J_n, X_{n-1}) S_i(Z_n, J_n, (X_{n-1}, b))$$

(5) The $U_i(Z_n, J_n, X_n)$ satisfy the following relationships:

(a) If $m(Z_n, J_n, X_{n-1}) \neq 0$ for some (k, z_n, j_n), then

$$
\begin{aligned}
U_i(Z_{n-1}, J_{n-1}, X_{n-1}) = \sum_{k, z_n, j_n} d_k(Z_n, J_n, X_{n-1})[t_k(Z_n, J_n, X_{n-1}) \\
- C_i(Z_n, J_n, X_{n-1}) + h(f_k(Z_n, J_n) \\
- t(Z_n, J_n, X_{n-1}))(U_i(Z_n, J_n, (X_{n-1}, a)) \\
- U_i(Z_n, J_n, (X_{n-1}, b)))) + U_i(Z_n, J_n, (X_{n-1}, b))]
\end{aligned}
$$

where the $d_k(Z_n, J_n, X_{n-1})$ are defined exactly as in the definition of equilibrium.

(b) If $m_k(Z_n, J_n, X_{n-1}) = 0$ for all (k, z_n, j_n), then
$U_i(Z_{n-1}, J_{n-1}, X_{n-1})$ belongs to the interval bounded by the maximum and minimum possible values of this variable.

This completes the definition of the correspondence A.

Now, every element in the vector (t, m, p, S) is mapped into a set which is either a point or a closed interval. Hence the image of every point is compact and convex. This leaves only upper semicontinuity. Assume that $(t^v, m^v, p^v, S^v) \rightarrow (\bar{t}, \bar{m}, \bar{p}, \bar{S})$ as $v \rightarrow \infty$, $(w^v, y^v, r^v, U^v) \in A(t^v, m^v, p^v, S^v)$, and $(w^v, y^v, r^v, U^v) \rightarrow (\bar{w}, \bar{y}, \bar{r}, \bar{U})$. We must show that $(\bar{w}, \bar{y}, \bar{r}, \bar{U}) \in A(\bar{t}, \bar{m}, \bar{p}, \bar{S})$. Most of the conditions defining A can be checked mechanically. Condition (1) is automatic. Conditions (2) and (3) are verified by considering two cases. If $\bar{m}_i(Z_n, J_n, X_{n-1}) = 0$ for all i, then the corresponding image sets for $\bar{w}(Z_n, J_n, X_{n-1})$ and $\bar{r}(a|Z_n, J_n, X_{n-1})$ are as large as possible, so that $\bar{w}(Z_n, J_n, X_{n-1})$ and $\bar{r}(a|Z_n, J_n, X_{n-1})$ must belong to them. Otherwise, the defining expressions in 2(a) and 2(b) are continuous, so that by taking limits, these variables are found to have the requisite values. Note, however, that the continuity of the function h is important. If, for example, $h(x) = 0$ for $x < 0$, $h(x) = 1$ for $x \geqq 0$ (the perfect accuracy case), then this argument would not hold.

The argument just given for conditions (2) and (3) applies to condition (5). This leaves only condition (4).

Suppose that $\bar{y}_i(Z_n, J_n, X_{n-1}) \neq 0$. Since $y_i^v(Z_n, J_n, X_{n-1}) \rightarrow y_i(Z_n, J_n, X_{n-1})$, it follows that there is a V, such that for all

$v > V$,

$$y_i^v(Z_n, J_n, X_{n-1}) \neq 0.$$

Since $(w^v, y^v, r^v, U^v) \; \epsilon \; A(t^v, m^v, p^v, S^v)$, it follows that (z_n, j_n) maximizes

$$t_i^v(Z_n, J_n, X_{n-1}) - c_i(Z_n, J_n, X_{n-1})$$
$$+ p^v(a|Z_n, J_n, X_{n-1})S_i^v(Z_n, J_n, (X_{n-1}, a))$$
$$+ p^v(b|Z_n, J_n, X_{n-1})S_i^v(Z_n, J_n, (X_{n-1}, b)).$$

It follows from letting $v \to \infty$ that (z_n, j_n) maximizes

$$\bar{t}_i(Z_n, J_n, X_{n-1}) - c_i(Z_n, J_n, X_{n-1})$$
$$+ \bar{p}(a|Z_n, J_n, X_{n-1})\bar{S}_i(Z_n, J_n, (X_{n-1}, a))$$
$$+ \bar{p}(b|Z_n, J_n, X_{n-1})\bar{S}_i(Z_n, J_n, (X_{n-1}, b)).$$

This is what we set out to show. Hence

$$(\bar{w}, \bar{y}, \bar{r}, \bar{U}) \; \epsilon \; A(\bar{t}, \bar{m}, \bar{p}, \bar{S}),$$

and A is upper semicontinuous.

The Kakutani fixed point theorem allows us to conclude that A has a fixed point, (t^*, m^*, p^*, S^*), which, by definition, is an equilibrium in the flow-through labor market system.

Comparison of the Static and Flow-through Models

The static model can be viewed as a time slice of the flow-through model. A group is defined by its initial type i and its history $(Z_{n-1}, J_{n-1}, X_{n-1})$. The signaling and job choice game in the nth period can be seen as a version of the static model for this group. Note that history, because it is observable and unalterable, is effectively an index. It separates this group off for signaling purposes.

A modified cost function for this group can be defined as follows.

$$C_i^*(z_n, j_n) = C_i(Z_n, J_n, X_{n-1})$$
$$+ p(a|Z_n, J_n, X_{n-1})S_i(Z_n, J_n, (X_{n-1}, a))$$
$$+ p(b|Z_n, J_n, X_{n-1})S_i(Z_n, J_n, (X_{n-1}, b))$$

Note that this cost function depends upon the equilibria in periods subsequent to n. Let

$$t_i^*(z_n, j_n) = t_i(Z_n, J_n, X_{n-1}).$$

The employee optimizing problem then is

$$\max_{z_n, j_n} [t_i(z_n, j_n) - C_i^*(z_n, j_n)].$$

The only difference between this and the static model is that offered wages depend on i here. The reason is that the individual has worked for some employers before and hence is not an anonymous quantity to those for whom he has worked. Ignoring history, it is as if some employers had privileged inside information about some individuals in the static model. This kind of inside information can easily be built into the static model, with no fundamental structural changes. Aside from the privileged information problem, employers react here as they do in the static model.

I would argue therefore, that the static model is usefully viewed as a time slice of the flow-through system. Histories are indices. Signaling costs are modified to include expected future benefits and costs of signaling and employment decisions now. Notice that the assertion is not that signaling equilibria in different periods in the flow-through model are independent. On the contrary, given the forward-looking investment aspects of employee decisions, they are fully interdependent. The static model, then, can be viewed as a way of getting at the structure of the market signaling game for some group at some point of time, taking the rest of the system (meaning the equilibrium configuration of the markets in other periods) as given.

My purpose in constructing the flow-through model was to buttress the static model by showing that it can be viewed as a representation of a time slice of an ongoing process. In so doing, I hope to have convinced the reader that some worrisome omissions in the static model (what happens when the employer learns about the individual's productive capabilities?) can be formally captured in an equilibrium model with the same basic structure as the static model.

Appendix J. Cooperative Behavior

The theory of coalitions and signaling is complicated and too involved to be dealt with adequately here. However, the following observation may be of some interest.

Proposition 1: If each type of individual can costlessly identify people of his own type, and if any coalition of people can costlessly and infallibly certify its members, having identified their type, then the resulting cooperative signaling game is inessential, and the single point in the core is the competitive equilibrium in a world of perfect information.

Remark: Note that only people of the same type can identify each other. The proposition may then be taken as saying that the usual competitive equilibrium can survive on something less than perfect information. Nevertheless, the assumption that people of the same type can identify each other is extreme and should be relaxed.

Proof: Let $q_i =$ the number of people of type i. People of type i can guarantee themselves at least

$$q_i \max_j (f_{ij} - c_{ij}),$$

by forming a certifying coalition. Since this is true of all types, and the maximum total return to the population is

$$\sum_i q_i \max_j (f_{ij} - c_{ij}),$$

each person of type i receives exactly $\max_{j}(f_{ij} - c_{ij})$. In a world of perfect information, each person of type i would optimally invest in the productive input j by maximizing $f_{ij} - c_{ij}$ with respect to j. Hence, the core of the cooperative game is the perfect information competitive equilibrium. |||

Bibliography

Akerlof, G. A. "The Market for 'Lemons': Qualitative Uncertainty and the Market Mechanism." *Quarterly Journal of Economics,* vol. 84, August 1970.

Allison, G. T. *Essence of Decision.* Boston: Little, Brown and Company, 1971.

Arrow, K. J. "Models of Discrimination." In A. H. Pascal, ed. *Racial Discrimination in Economic Life.* Lexington, Mass.: D. C. Heath, 1972.

————. *Theory of Risk-Bearing.* Chicago: Markham Publishing Company, 1971.

Becker, G. *The Economics of Discrimination.* Chicago: University of Chicago Press, 1957.

Berg, Ivar. *Education and Jobs: The Great Training Robbery.* Boston: Beacon Press, 1971.

Bogess, William. "Screen Test Your Credit Risks." *Harvard Business Review,* November 1967.

Burkill, J. C. *The Theory of Ordinary Differential Equations.* Edinburgh: Oliver and Boyd Ltd., 1956.

Calibresi, G. "Does the Fault System Optimally Control Primary Accident Costs?" *Law and Contemporary Problems,* Duke University School of Law, Durham, N.C., summer 1968.

Caywood, Thomas E. "Point Scoring for Credit Customers." *Banking,* October 1970.

Chiswick, Barry R. "Schooling, Screening, and Income." Mimeographed, National Bureau of Economic Research, March 1972.

Debreu, G. *The Theory of Value.* Cowles Foundation Monograph no. 17. New York: John Wiley and Sons, Inc., 1959.

————, and H. Scarf. "A Limit Theorem on the Core of an Economy." *International Economic Review,* September 1963.

Doeringer, P., and M. Piore. *Internal Labor Markets and Manpower Analysis.* Boston: D. C. Heath, 1971.

Feller, W. *Introduction to Probability Theory and Its Applications,* vol. I. New York: John Wiley and Sons, Inc., 1950.

Goffman, E. *Stigma.* Englewood Cliffs, N.J.: Prentice-Hall, Inc., 1963.

————. *Strategic Interaction.* Philadelphia: University of Pennsylvania Press, 1969.

Goldman, D. *Information Theory.* New York: Dover Publications, Inc., 1968.

Green, J. "The Nature and Existence of Stochastic Equilibria." Mimeographed, Harvard University, October 1970.

————. "Stochastic Equilibrium: A Stability Theorem and Application." The Economics Series, Institute for Mathematical Studies in the Social Sciences, Technical Report no. 46, Stanford University, August 1971.

Hahn, F., and K. J. Arrow. *General Competitive Analysis.* San San Francisco: Holden Day, Inc., 1971.

Hirshleifer, J. "The Private and Social Value of Information and the Reward to Inventive Activity." *American Economic Review,* vol. 61, September 1971.

Hull, S., and L. Peter. *The Peter Principle.* New York: Bantam Press, 1969.

Jervis, R. *The Logic of Images in International Relations.* Princeton: Princeton University Press, 1970.

Johnson, Nicholas. "How Point Scoring Can Do More Than Help Make Loan Decisions." *Banking,* August 1971.

Kain, J., ed. *Race and Poverty.* Englewood Cliffs, N.J.: Prentice-Hall, Inc., 1969.

Kakutani, S. "A Generalization of Brouwer's Fixed Point Theorem." *Duke Mathematics Journal,* vol. 8, 1941.

Kemeny, J. G., and J. L. Snell. *Finite Markov Chains.* Princeton, N.J.: Van Nostrand, 1960.

La Decision: Aggregation et dynamique des ordres des preferences. Centre National de la Recherche Scientifique, Aix-en-Provence, July 3–7, 1967.

Lewis, D. K. *Convention: A Philosophical Study.* Cambridge, Mass.: Harvard University Press, 1969.

Lorenz, K. *On Aggression.* New York: Harcourt, Brace and World, Inc., 1963.

Luce, D., and H. Raiffa. *Games and Decisions.* New York: John Wiley and Sons, Inc., 1957.

McCall, J. J. "Racial Discrimination in the Job Market: The Role of Information and Search," RAND Memorandum RM–6162–OEO, January 1970.

McGuire, C. B., and R. Radner, eds. *Decision and Organization: A Volume in Honor of Jacob Marschak.* Amsterdam: North Holland, 1972.

Marschak, J. "Remarks on the Economics of Information." In *Contributions to Scientific Research in Management,* Western Data Processing Center. Los Angeles: University of California, 1959.

Miller, Arthur R. *The Assault on Privacy.* Ann Arbor: University of Michigan Press, 1971.

Myrdal, G. *An American Dilemma: The Negro Problem and Modern Democracy.* New York: Harper and Brothers, 1944.

Nelson, Phillip. "Advertising as Information." Mimeographed, State University of New York at Stonybrook, N.Y., July 1972.

————. "Information and Consumer Behavior." *Journal of Political Economy,* vol. 78, March-April 1970.

Olson, M. *The Logic of Collective Action.* New York: Schocken Books, 1968.

Oniki, H. "Communication Costs of Operating Organizations." Unpublished paper presented at the Econometric Society Meetings, New Orleans, December 1971.

Pascal, A. H., and L. A. Rapping. "Racial Discrimination in Organized Baseball." In A. H. Pascal, ed. *Racial Discrimination in Economic Life.* Lexington, Mass.: D. C. Heath, 1972.

Phelps, E. S. "Profitable Discrimination: The Statistical Theory of 'Racism' and 'Sexism'." Mimeographed, Columbia University, May 1971.

Pratt, J. "Risk Aversion in the Small and in the Large." *Econometrica,* vol. 32, January 1964.

Pratt, J., H. Raiffa, R. Schlaifer. *Introduction to Statistical Decision Theory.* New York: McGraw-Hill, 1965.

Radner, R. "Competitive Equilibrium Under Uncertainty." *Econometrica,* vol. 36, January 1968.

Raiffa, H. *Decision Analysis*. Reading, Mass.: Addison-Wesley, 1968.

————, and R. Schlaifer. *Applied Statistical Decision Theory*. Cambridge, Mass.: The M.I.T. Press, 1961.

Rothschild, M. "The Persistence of Error: A Useful Fact About Two-Armed Bandit Problems." Mimeographed, Harvard University, September 1971.

————. "Models of Market Organization with Imperfect Information." Harvard Institute of Economic Research, Discussion paper no. 224, December 1971, forthcoming in the *Journal of Political Economy*.

Samuelson, P. A. *The Foundations of Economic Analysis*. Cambridge, Mass.: Harvard University Press, 1947.

Scarf, H. "On the Existence of a Cooperative Solution for a General Class of N-Person Gamer." Cowles Foundation, Discussion paper no. 293, New Haven, April 1970.

————. "The Core of an N-Person Game." *Econometrica*, vol. 35, January 1967.

Schelling, T. C. *Strategy of Conflict*. New York: Oxford University Press, 1963.

————. "Models of Segregation." RAND Memorandum RM–6014–RC, May 1969.

————. "Neighborhood Tipping." Harvard Institute of Economic Research, Discussion paper no. 100, December 1969.

————. "Ecology of Micromotives." J. F. Kennedy School of Government, Harvard University, Discussion paper no. 3, December 1969.

Spence, A. M., and R. J. Zeckhauser. "Insurance, Information, and Individual Action." *American Economic Review, Papers and Proceedings,* vol. 61, May 1971.

Starr, R. M. "Quasi-Equilibria in Markets with Non-Convex Preferences." *Econometrica*, vol. 37, January 1969.

Thurow, L. *Poverty and Discrimination*. Washington, D.C.: The Brookings Institution, 1969.

Vaquin, Michael. "The Economics of Information in Insurance Markets." Mimeographed, Harvard University, August 1972.

Weiner, N. *Cybernetics or Control and Communication in the Animal and the Machine*. Cambridge, Mass.: The M.I.T. Press, 1948.

Weiss, R. D. "The Effect of Education on the Earnings of Blacks and Whites." *Review of Economics and Statistics,* vol. 52, May 1970.

Wheat, David. "A Consideration of the Disproportionately Large Percentage of Black Arrestees." Mimeographed, J. F. Kennedy School of Government, Harvard University, November 1971.

Zeckhauser, R. J. *Microeconomic Interdependence.* Unpublished manuscript, Harvard University, October 1969.

————. "Medical Insurance: A Case Study of the Tradeoff between Risk Spreading and Appropriate Incentives." *Journal of Economic Theory,* vol. 2, March 1970.

————. "Markets Where Sellers Are Searchers." Mimeographed, J. F. Kennedy School of Government, Harvard University, June 1972.

Index